Information Systems
Project Management

Information Systems Project Management

David L. Olson
University of Nebraska—Lincoln

BUSINESS EXPERT PRESS

Information Systems Project Management
Copyright © Business Expert Press, LLC, 2015.

First published in 2015 by
Business Expert Press, LLC
222 East 46th Street, New York, NY 10017
www.businessexpertpress.com

ISBN-13: 978-1-63157-122-0 (paperback)
ISBN-13: 978-1-63157-123-7 (e-book)

Business Expert Press Consumer Behavior Collection

Collection ISSN: 2156-8189 (print)
Collection ISSN: 2156-8200 (electronic)

Cover and interior design by S4Carlisle Publishing Services
Private Ltd., Chennai, India

First edition: 2015

10 9 8 7 6 5 4 3 2 1

Printed in the United States of America.

Table of Contents

Preface

This book addresses project management in the context of information systems. It deals with general project management principles, with focus on the special characteristics of information systems. It is based on an earlier text,[1] but shortened to focus on essential project management elements.

An introductory chapter discusses project features in general. The systems perspective provides a useful framework for project analysis. The systems view is a concept useful for better understanding project purposes. Systems theory is important in project management because of the unintended consequences often encountered in projects due to complex interrelationships of system components. By viewing projects as systems, some of these unintended consequences may be anticipated, and prepared for.

Part I of the book focuses attention on the important human element in information systems projects. Chapter 2 is new, concerning human factors in information systems projects. Getting people to work toward the same ends is key to the success of any group activity. Even though information systems projects involve many technical matters, the human element continues to be critical. Chapter 3 discusses project organizational structure. Alternative forms of organization are discussed, focusing on those that have been successfully applied to project management. The abilities of various alternative organizational forms to deal with project uncertainty are discussed.

Part II discusses two processes involved in the initial project definition stage. Chapter 4 discusses issues concerning the adoption of proposed projects. A number of quantitative methods are demonstrated, including multiple objective analysis. Chapter 5 discusses systems development options.

Part III involves planning. The planning stage involves specific identification of how projects are going to be accomplished. Chapter 6 reviews project estimation practice. Some of the quantitative methods used are demonstrated. Chapter 7 presents and demonstrates deterministic critical path methods, and discusses resource leveling and constraining.

Part V deals with project implementation. Chapter 8 discusses project control features, and means of assessing project success. Techniques to deal with a variety of risks involved in software project development are reviewed. Project implementation issues are examined in Chapter 9, including detailed discussion of critical success factors.

A feature of the book is an effort to tie content to that of the Project Management Body of Knowledge (PMBOK).[2] Each chapter includes reference to how each chapter relates to the PMBOK structure.

References

1   D.L. Olson. 2004. *Introduction to Information Systems Project Management* (Englewood Cliffs, NJ: McGraw-Hill/Irwin).

2   Project Management Institute. 2013. *Guide to the Project Management Body of Knowledge (PMBOK Guide)* (Newtown Square, PA: PMI).

CHAPTER 1

Introduction to Project Management

Almost every organization gets involved in many projects. A major reason projects are so important is the fast pace of change, and the more specialized nature of modern business. Many of these projects involve information systems, a distinctive type of project. Firms have to keep at least close to the cutting edge for harnessing the power of computers in almost every aspect of business. Large accounting firms have enlarged their information system consulting operations, and almost all of this type of consulting involves an information systems project. This means that there are more and more unique activities drawing people together from diverse locations and diverse organizations with diverse, specialized skills.

Project management has long been associated with operations management, and is an important topic in operations management's curriculum. There has been an explosion of projects in the field of information systems. Information systems project management involves some characteristics different from those found in operations management, but many of the same tools can be applied. This is due primarily to the volume of new projects to implement computer technology that organizations have adopted. There are many useful things that information technology can do for organizations. The information technology environment involves high turnover of personnel, turbulent work environments, and rapidly changing technology. This results in high levels of uncertainty with respect to time and cost. Despite this more volatile environment, project management principles applicable to operations management can often be transferred to the information system environment.

What Is a Project?

A project involves getting a new, complex activity accomplished. Many activities qualify as projects. Building the Golden Gate Bridge, transporting the Statue of Liberty across the Atlantic, and the attempt to elect Mitt Romney President were all major projects. So were the development of the atomic bomb and sending men to the moon.

Each political campaign is a marketing project, just like other marketing projects to sell new products. You have each written a paper, which was assigned as a "project." These projects involved researching some topic, and organizing ideas into a cohesive, rational whole. In football, developing a promising young quarterback prospect is often a multiyear project, including intensive coaching to learn the team's offense, to learn the style of teammates, development of leadership skills, passing technique, and building endurance and strength. What television viewers might view as natural talent may have involved the closely planned and coordinated activities of quite a large number of people.

Projects:

- Involve a definable purpose
- Cut across organizational lines
- Are unique activities.

Projects are purposeful, in that they are designed to accomplish something for the organization undertaking them. Projects usually cut across organizational lines, drawing people from a variety of functional specialties. Constructing automobiles on an assembly line is no longer a project once the assembly line is developed, because it becomes a closed, repetitive activity that continues as long as anyone can foresee. Making a series of sales calls is not a project, because it is not a unique activity. However, just like the first assembly line, the first round of sales calls is a project, until a desired level of competence is attained. Projects include:

- Constructing something
  - a road, a dam, a building, an information system
- Organizing something
  - a meeting, an election campaign, a symphony, a movie

- Doing anything the first time is a project
- Accomplishing a new, complex activity.

Project Characteristics

Because projects involve new activities, they typically involve high levels of uncertainty and risk. One of the reasons assembly line operations are efficient is that everyone does the same thing over and over, hour after hour, day after day, year after year. This repetitiveness allows high degrees of specialization, which in turn enables greater productivity. The activities of many different people and machines can be balanced for maximum efficiency in an assembly line operation. **Projects involve lower degrees of efficiency** than are obtained in assembly line operations.

Because of this higher degree of uncertainty, it is much more difficult to estimate the level of resources required to accomplish a project than it is for other forms of productive organizations. It is also more difficult to estimate the time required (which amounts to another resource). Many projects are late, but not all projects take longer than estimated. The Russian atomic bomb project was completed ahead of schedule, and about the same time, the U.S. U-2 airplane project was finished in about one-tenth of the estimated time. Yet, projects finished ahead of schedule are still rare. **Projects are collections of activities**. If one activity is late, other activities often have to wait for it to finish. If an activity is ahead of schedule, those doing the work tend to be more careful, or slow down for other reasons. Following activities often cannot start early anyway, as the people and materials for following activities may not be available until the originally scheduled starting time. For these and other reasons, it is far more common for projects to be late than to be finished early.

Because of their temporary nature, projects inevitably involve gathering together a diverse group of specialists to accomplish a variety of tasks. Project team members often will not know each other very well, at least in the beginning of the project. They will tend to be quite different people, with different skill sets and interests. The primary feature of a project is that it is a **set of temporary activities conducted by ad hoc organizations**.

Information systems projects have many similarities to generic projects. They consist of activities, each with durations, predecessor relationships, and resource requirements. They involve high levels of uncertainty and often suffer from time and cost overruns, while rarely experiencing time and cost underruns. However, information systems projects are different from generic projects in some aspects. While each project is unique, there are usually many, many replications of information system project types. Most are served by a standard methodology, with the need to identify user requirements, followed by design of a system, production of the system, testing of the system, training and implementation, and ultimately maintenance of the system. These steps are not always serial, with many loops back to prior stages. They involve the need for specialists in different areas of the information system field, but these specialties are not as distinctly different as carpentry and electrical work. Systems analysts usually know how to program, and testers know all of the other functions involved in a project. Project team members from the development side usually understand each other well. Information systems projects of course involve computers, which is a distinct characteristic that has more impact than initially might be apparent.

Information Systems Projects

Projects in the engineering world tend to involve a lot of uncertainty (especially with respect to how long they will take). But information systems projects have added levels of uncertainty. To demonstrate these differences, let us consider four types of projects: engineering (construction), political, movies, and information systems.

First, engineering projects involve more physical activities, while the other three types of projects involve people creating something. It can be argued that engineering projects are thus much easier to manage, because scheduling is a matter of calculating physical quantities and using past production rates to determine how long activities should take.

Second, information systems projects require specialists in different skill sets to work together to create a software product. Movies are similar in this respect. There may be some variety in skills needed in political projects, but for the most part it is public relations—working with the press to put your candidate in the best light, and get maximum positive exposure. (Some specialists may be needed to cover up negative exposures.) Information systems and movies involve lots of different specialties. Movies need actors, a staff to make actors happy, camera people, directors, grips, and lots of other things. Information systems projects need system analysts, programmers and/or software developers, testers, system installers, trainers, and other specialty skills.

Third, projects involving humans creating things are much more difficult to estimate, because it is more difficult to estimate how long a creative activity (like writing a bug-free code) will take. Actually, political campaigns are more predictable because there is an end point—voting day. Effectiveness might be hard to estimate, but duration is pretty much given. Movies also have planned schedules, but directors may feel that artistic creativity was lacking in scheduled shots, and insist on redoing them. Information systems clearly involve less certainty as to duration than the other three kinds of projects considered here.

Dimensions of Complexity

Projects can differ on a number of aspects. These include the number of people involved, and the diversity of skills involved. Some projects are individual efforts to accomplish something. Others, like a major military campaign, can involve hundreds of thousands of people. The more people that are involved, the greater the need to organize into subunits, requiring a higher proportion of managers and thus a lower proportion of productive people. In general, the more complex the project, the more time and resources that are required.

Group size dimensions can vary over extremes. A few examples of projects for different sized groups, ranging from individual effort through three general group levels, are given for comparison.

Projects can also differ on the dimensions of uncertainty. It is much more difficult to predict how much time is going to be required the first time you do something. Since projects are usually things done for the first time, they usually take longer than expected when they were estimated. Information systems currently are in very high demand, outstripping their supply. Another possible bias is introduced by the practice of

Project Size by Size of Group	
Individual:	A term paper is often an individual effort.
	Making an oil painting of a landscape is an individual project.
Group:	Organizing a wedding can be a major project for a small group
	Implementing a computer system may involve a small group project
	Each audit is a project conducted by auditing specialists.
Organization:	Construction organizations are created to develop efficient skills at building structures of one type or another. As each project is completed, there is often a great deal of change in personnel, although the organization will retain some of its people for the next project.
	Information systems consulting organizations follow a similar pattern.
Multiorganization:	The space shuttle involves coordinated activities of many people.
	Probably the most involved projects known to mankind are also the most wasteful. World War II involved the radical reorganization of entire countries, relocation of entire industries in the Soviet Union, long marches in China, the rebuilding of entire industries in Germany and England, and development of entire new industries in the United States.

making initial estimates intentionally low to get work. This bias improves the probability of getting work, which is often negotiated on a cost-plus basis. This practice is not at all recommended, as it leads to a bad reputation when initial promises are not kept. Furthermore, it has ethical ramifications with respect to truth in advertising. An additional factor in project lateness is that large government projects are the most commonly reported. These projects tend to be very complex, and often run over in time and budget. How many times have you read about a government project of significant magnitude taking less time than estimated? Since there is a strong correlation between time and money, late projects almost always cost more than expected. When was the last time you heard of a government project having a cost underrun?

General project management is a field that has developed primarily since World War II. With more complex undertakings, many project management principles have developed. They typically involve a cost/time/quality tradeoff, found in almost any project. Specifically in the information systems field, this tradeoff can be stated as follows:

In the field of information systems, there is an old adage that you can have any two of three things in a project. You can get it done on time, you can get it done within budgeted cost, or you can get it done well. If you are willing to wait, you can get the job done right within cost. If you are willing to spend the money, you can get a good job done quickly. Or, you can get the job done on time and within budget, with the only reservation being that it will not perform as specified.

This adage is not presented as a recommended way to treat all projects. We all like to think that we can do better than anyone else, and accomplish all three tasks. But over and over, in the fields of construction, government projects, and in information systems, problems in completing projects on time, within budget, and meeting specifications have been encountered. Project management cannot be blamed for all of these reported failures. The point is that we should understand the difficulties involved in a project environment, seeking to understand the project as a system so that we keep it on target with respect to accomplishing what it is intended to do, in the most timely and efficient manner possible. Bringing in a project on time, within budget, and meeting specifications is tough. Project managers need to expect difficult challenges.

Modern Business

Business has grown much more complex, with interrelated currencies and stock markets. The pace of business is at the speed of light, as stock trading is conducted electronically, oftentimes by artificial intelligence systems. Information technology markets are less predictable. The outputs of many companies are tied together through just-in-time systems with dedicated suppliers. At the output end of production, producers and retailers are often connected through electronic data interchange. The international aspect of business is typified by new arrangements such as GATT, NAFTA, and the European Economic Community. The rapid pace of change has resulted in the disappearance of many companies, age-old organizations like the Southwest Conference, and entire countries like the Soviet Union.

In the rapidly changing world of business today, there is a growing need to manage projects intelligently. Project management advanced a great deal in the defense, aerospace, and construction industries. Techniques developed for controlling the interrelated activities of many different organizations and crews can be applied to the field of information systems, which includes many projects to install new applications, or to tie old applications together.

Viewing Projects as Systems

Systems are collections of interrelated parts working together to accomplish one or more objectives. There are many systems of interacting parts where viewing the whole tells us more than simply looking at the system's components. In systems, output is not simply the sum of component parts. Components are affected by other parts of the system. System components are affected by being in the system, and the sum of the system output is greater than what the sum of individual outputs would have been without being in the system. Systems are purposeful, meant to do something.

Project Management Systems

Information projects are systems. Subsystems found in project management systems include a technical core, a control subsystem, and a project information subsystem. The **technical core** includes the technical expertise and equipment that gives the system the ability to accomplish what it needs to do. Expertise can include systems analysis, program development, testing, installation, and user training skills. Equipment in a broad sense can include software, such as CASE tools and subroutines that improve productivity. The **control subsystem** is the means management has to control operations. Within an organization, this control subsystem coordinates the technical core with the outside environment. In an institution, an example of a control subsystem is the board of directors, which approves goals and strategies for the organization (which are usually generated by top management). In a project management system, control includes procedures specified for specific tasks, milestones to mark completion of project phases, and the expertise available within the project team to solve problems when they are encountered. The **project information subsystem** gives management measures of how the system is accomplishing its objectives. Project information systems need to record the current status of activities, list responsibilities, planned and actual durations of activities, and cost expenditures.

The value of viewing information systems projects as systems is that the total view of the project in light of its intended purpose is clearer. Projects consist of many interrelated tasks, done by different people with different skills. If each task was accomplished in isolation, many suboptimalities would occur. Possibly specific tasks would be done faster or at less expense if the rest of the project was disregarded, but the focus of each member of the project team should be to accomplish project objectives, and not to optimize production of specific tasks. If tradeoffs exist between task accomplishment and project accomplishment, the systems view makes it clear that overall project considerations come first.

Systems provide a useful framework within which to view projects. To make projects work, project managers need to be able to anticipate the consequences of planned actions. They need to develop a system organization, through hiring and training appropriate, qualified people, within budget. They need to be able to know who they have to deal with outside of the system, for supplies, materials, regulation compliance, etc. They need to understand how to measure how the project is going, and what controls are available if the project is not going as planned. Understanding the concept of systems makes it much easier to see the impact of the principles of project management.

Project Entities

A number of people are needed to make projects work. We have stated that user involvement is important. One reason is that they are the client (**stakeholders**). The client paying for or controlling the project is the **sponsor** (sometimes appearing in the form of a **project board**), causing the project to be undertaken. Related to the sponsor is the **project champion** (sometimes another synonym for sponsor). A project champion may not have authority, but has influence at the budgetary authorizing level, and often serves as a cheerleader in keeping top management support for the project high.

The **project manager** coordinates the efforts of people coming from a variety of functional areas. Project managers also need to integrate planning and control costs, by assigning tasks and schedules to the members of the project team.

The **project team** is a group of people with the required skills to accomplish the project. They will often come from different places with radically different skills and backgrounds. Oftentimes these project team members will enter the project (and leave) at different times, making for an even greater degree of turbulence. People who work on projects need to be very flexible, and to learn to work with a variety of other people.

The **project management system** is the organizational structure used by the project manager to get things done. The project management system includes the information system to provide project team members with necessary information, as coordination between groups is critical to integrate activities. Organizational structure involves procedures to ensure accurate communication and completeness of activities.

The Information System Project Environment

Successful implementation has been found to require mastery of the technical aspects of systems along with understanding of key organizational and behavioral dynamics. There has been a great deal of study of information system **project failure**. Failure can arise due to failing to meet design objectives. Projects also can fail with respect to time and budget constraints. Seemingly successful projects may fail because their intended users do not use them. And finally, systems may not meet the expectations of stakeholders.

Most information systems projects have been reported to be much less successful, reflecting in part a very turbulent environment where many changes are needed.[1] Quite often, management gives up and changes direction. This is not always possible to do.

A great deal of study has been given to factors that lead to project success. These factors include planning, user involvement, good communication, and sound monitoring of projects. Additional factors that repeatedly are reported as important in information system project success include top management support and clear statement of project objectives.

Three factors have consistently appeared as success factors in information systems project failure. These factors, also found in general kinds of projects, are:

> Client involvement
> Top management support
> Clear statement of project objectives

Summary

Project management has many features different from those of repetitive operations. These include:

- Lower degrees of efficiency
- Operating in a much less predictable market with more rapidly changing technology
- The need to coordinate more parties and organizations
- A highly dynamic environment involving temporary tasks.

Information systems project management has its own unique features. The market for information systems products is growing very rapidly, but is also extremely volatile. Each year sees radical new opportunities to harness computer technology to do our jobs better, and for business to be conducted in better ways. But this means that we must constantly expect change, and we need to keep mastering new skills.

Projects are systems consisting of interrelated parts working together to accomplish project objectives. There are a number of important roles within information systems projects. Project managers have to balance technical understanding with the ability to motivate diverse groups of people (the project team) brought together on a temporary basis. Managing this team requires organizing in a way that groups can coordinate their diverse activities. Project champions play an important role in obtaining organizational commitment to projects.

While there are many valuable information systems projects that have been completed, the development environment is very difficult. Rarely do information systems projects finish on time, within budget, and fulfill specifications simultaneously. Top management support to projects has repeatedly been found to be critical to information systems project success. User groups need to be consulted to find out just what systems will be required to do. Systems designers need to be involved to make sure that new systems fit in with the overall organizational information system. Programmers need to be involved to ensure realistic production rates. End users need to be involved to ensure the quality of systems by making sure that they are usable and useful. After planning is completed, there need to be many meetings to coordinate the project through completion and acceptance.

This book is based on an earlier text,[2] but shortened to focus on essential project management elements. This chapter has presented various statistics indicating endemic problems in completing information system projects on time, within budget, at designed functionality. While successful completion of an information systems project is a challenge, there are some things that can be done to improve the probability of project success. This book reviews a number of project management tools. These include developing organizational ability to work on projects, discussed in Chapters 2 and 3. Sponsor expectations can be based upon better information if a good job of project selection is conducted, discussed in Chapter 4. Better systems analysis and design (Chapter 5) and project estimation (covered in Chapter 6) can assure that the proper skills are acquired to develop the project. Project management tools (Chapter 7) can assist project managers in coordinating the project effort, as can project management software such as Microsoft Project. Chapter 8 will return to the importance of critical success factors in the context of project implementation. Chapter 9 will discuss project control and termination.

Glossary

Control subsystem: Means by which project management directs project activities.

Project: A unique, one-time activity to develop something new.

Project board: Management group causing the project to be undertaken (synonyms: sponsor, stakeholders).

Project champion: One who sponsors a project and performs the role of maintaining organizational support for it.

Project failure: Failure of the project to be completed on time, within budget, and with designed functionality. In a stricter sense, failure of the product of the project to be used, or failure of the project results to meet stakeholder expectations.

Project information subsystem: System to inform project management of objective accomplishment and progress.

Project management system: Organizational structure available to the project manager with which the project can be successfully completed (in a more specific sense, computer software to aid in managing a project).

Project manager: Individual assigned responsibility for accomplishing project objectives.

Project team: Personnel (consisting of the diverse set of skills required) assigned to accomplish the project.

Sponsor: Entity that caused the project to be undertaken, and who arranged for payment.

Stakeholders: Organizational members affected by the project (includes sponsors, users, and project team).

System: A collection entities responsible for accomplishment of interrelated activities with a common purpose.

Technical core: Expertise and equipment required to successfully complete a project.

"We will provide links to the PMBOK, Project Management Body of Knowledge, in each chapter."

PMBOK Items Relating to Chapter 1:

1.2 A project is a temporary endeavor undertaken to create a unique product, service, or result.

   1.2.1 A portfolio refers to a collection of projects, programs, subportfolios, and operations managed as a group to achieve strategic objectives.

1.3 Project management is the application of knowledge, skills, tools, and techniques to project activities to meet project requirements.

   1.4.1 A program is defined as a group of related projects, subprograms, and program activities managed in a coordinated way to obtain benefits not available from managing them individually.

1.4.2 A portfolio refers to projects, programs, subportfolios, and operations managed as a group to achieve strategic objectives.

2.1.5 Enterprise environmental factors refer to conditions, not under the control of the project team, that influence, constrain, or direct the project.

2.2 A stakeholder is an individual, group, or organization who may affect, be affected by a decision, activity, or outcome of a project.

2.2.1 Stakeholders include all members of the project team as well as all interested entities that are internal or external to the organization.

13.1 Identify Stakeholders—process of identifying the people, groups, or organizations that could impact or be impacted by a decision, activity, or outcome of the project; and analyzing and documenting relevant information regarding their interests, involvement, interdependencies, influence, and potential impact on project success.

13.2 Plan Stakeholder Management—process of developing appropriate management strategies to effectively engage stakeholders throughout the project life cycle, based on the analysis of their needs, interests, and potential impact on project success.

13.3 Manage Stakeholder Engagement—process of communicating and working with stakeholders to meet their needs/expectations, address issues as they occur, and foster appropriate stakeholder engagement in project activities throughout the project life cycle.

13.4 Control Stakeholder Engagement—process of monitoring overall project stakeholder relationships and adjusting strategies and plans for engaging stakeholders.

References

1 P. Simon. 2010. *Why New Systems Fail: An Insider's Guide to Successful IT Projects* (Independence, KY: Cengage Learning).

2 D.L. Olson. 2004. *Introduction to Information Systems Project Management* (Englewood Cliffs, NJ: McGraw-Hill/Irwin).

PART I

The Human Element

CHAPTER 2

Human Factors in Information Systems Project Management

A great deal of the effort involved in making a computer software project work is to get the project development team to work together. This is often difficult, because many computer software developers view life much like engineers and scientists. Their emphasis focuses on getting computers to work. Computers have no feelings, and do exactly what they are told. This environment leads to those people sometimes using a rather abrupt and curt mode of communication. Their ability to communicate effectively with humans is occasionally curtailed. Effective management of teams of software developers requires understanding both their personal tendencies, as well as those of users, usually a quite different personality type.

Information systems projects involve the need to coordinate the efforts of a diverse group of people. One of the most difficult (but also one of the most lucrative) jobs in the world right now is information system project management. These people have very high-pressure jobs, with a lot of demands upon them, and they tend to have a lot of turnover. However, project managers with experience are paid very well.

Information Systems Project Features

Information systems projects promise a great deal of benefit to organizations. There are many kinds of information systems projects. Enterprise resource planning (ERP) systems are very large scale, possibly centralizing all information systems support for an organization. ERP systems can be built in-house, but usually are purchased software systems. Installation of an ERP is a very large project, often involving interorganizational elements

Table 2.1 Waterfall model of software development with systems personnel

Stage	Personnel
System feasibility analysis	**Systems analysts**, users, finance
Software plans and requirements	**Systems analysts**, users
Product design	**Systems analysts**
Detailed design	**Systems analysts**
Coding	**Programmers, testing**
Integration	**Systems analysts, programmers, testers, systems administrators**
Implementation	**Systems administrators, testers**, users
Operations and maintenance	**Maintenance**

Information systems personnel titles in bold.

(including vendor and consultant personnel), but little systems development and programming. Web systems are at the other extreme. They are very useful means of implementing e-commerce and e-business (and other e-whatever), but usually are small scale, and can be turned over to one specialist who does everything. (There may be good reasons to have a team specialize on developing many websites, and there is a definite need to work with users.) Conventional information systems projects often consist of a series of development activities, referred to as a **waterfall model** (see Table 2.1) because if all goes well, results of prior stages spill down to the next stage. (In reality, a great deal of looping back is encountered.)

   Systems analysts have the job of identifying what the needs of the system are, and then designing an appropriate software product. This involves the need to understand business problems and to talk to business users, as well as the ability to understand the technical domain and to talk to computer personnel. **Programmers** are usually specialists who talk to computers, and make them function. They can do a more complete job if they talk to humans as well, but some specialize. Testers are very important personnel who try their best to find flaws in systems. Sometimes testers obtain character traits reflecting this critical attitude, but in order to do their job well, they need to be very meticulous. Systems administrators have the job of implementing software on server systems. This tends to be even more computer-centric than programming. Maintenance personnel are responsible for fixing bugs that are encountered, as well as keeping systems up to date with hardware and software system changes.

There are other information systems job titles as well. For instance, there are workers in database management, in providing help to users, in linking networks together, and many other specialties. Some of these may well be involved in specific projects. But generically, Table 2.1 lists the primary information system specialists found in conventional information systems projects.

Working in this environment, regardless of job title, is very interesting and can be very rewarding. However, it can also be very frustrating. There is a need to not only be technically competent, but also to be able to work with a variety of types of people. There is a need to work with users, who have problems that computer systems hopefully will solve. There is also a need to work with technical people, varying from systems administrators through coders and testers.

Individual characteristics are the result of different personalities, of individuals with different demographic backgrounds as well as education, and experience. These different people find themselves in different organizational roles, with different status levels. Individuals also have different psychological makeup, in the form of needs, interests, and goals. Within information systems project teams, a specific type of personality tends to predominate, focused on technical matters. But members of these project teams need to work with users, who tend to have psychological characteristics more common to the general public, focused on dealing with people, with a broader organizational focus.

Being part of a **project team** can lead to conflict. The degree of conflict is expected to depend upon team size, heterogeneity, and leadership. The larger the team, the more likely for some conflicts to arise, although it can be possible for antagonists to avoid each other in larger teams. The more diverse the team, the more likely conflicts are to arise. Within information systems teams, there tends to be a common technical focus, except for those whose specialty is training. However, sometimes having too many shared interests can lead to conflict, as there can be different opinions about how to proceed technically, and individuals may feel that other people are not competent, whereas in actuality they may simply have a different technical approach. Team processes can play a role in conflict, through the ability to communicate efficiently, and through the relative degree of participation encouraged. Team history may well play a major role in conflict. Working together in the past is usually viewed as a positive factor in conflict, but can be the worst case if personalities clashed in previous project efforts.

Characteristics of projects can also lead to greater levels of conflict. A major factor is time pressure. Some people thrive under pressure, others react adversely. Projects often involve pressures. They also often involve constraints, in that the ideal level of resources may not be available. Some people find that unacceptable, and refuse to proceed with project efforts. Others cope somehow. The more flexible approach is usually more productive. Other factors include success criteria (expectations) and top management support. Without top support, projects tend to be starved for resources, making the work environment difficult.

Organizational characteristics can also be important. Matrix organizations (to be discussed in Chapter 3) involve a very hectic kind of environment, highly suitable for information systems projects. However, it may not be suitable for specific individuals. In matrix organizations, there is a need for actors to quickly adapt to new circumstances, and to deal with new people, new responsibilities, and in general, be able to prosper in a highly dynamic environment. If this is not the type of working climate desired by a specific individual, that individual should find one of the many other professional fields to work in.

Interpersonal conflict can manifest itself in at least four levels. **Interdependence** is the process of people working together, realizing that their success depends on the cooperation of others. This is the form of team unity most desirable in an information systems project team. There will always be disagreements that arise. This is healthy, and reflects thought and effort applied by team members. (If there were no disagreements, this is an indication that some of the team members don't care.) The process of interpersonal conflict becomes disruptive if interference results, from disagreements escalating into actions taken to force one position at the expense of another. A higher level of conflict arises when negative emotions arise, as in heated arguments.

There are a number of different management styles available for team leaders to cope with interpersonal conflict. These styles include problem solving, compromising, asserting, accommodating, and avoiding. The appropriate style depends upon circumstances. Only by understanding human behavior can team leaders learn which style is needed. This selection can be an important factor in project success, system success, individual performance, and effective organizational performance.

Conflict and Performance

Conflict management is essential in obtaining positive information systems project outcomes. Conflict can be useful, in generating better solutions, but harmful behavior is counterproductive in any environment. The bottom line of this result is that it is better to avoid interpersonal conflict in the first place rather than rely upon project leadership ability to mitigate it. Features that might improve information system project success include:

1. **Project scope and objectives communicated to all of the project team**

   Management often feels that once a project is officially adopted, everyone should automatically rally behind it. They therefore omit detailed explanation of what the project is designed to do for the organization. This often leads to some resistance to the project by those who were not consulted in the decision, especially those who feel that their input would have been important.

   A related issue is the scope of the project. If the project scope is not clear to everyone, those who make decisions related to the project will not be in a position to make the best decisions. Additionally, user requirements need to have assurance that they are feasible. This is easier to assess if clearly stated acceptance criteria are present. Every requirement should include a definition of what makes the system performance acceptable.

2. **Business rationale for undertaking a project disseminated**

   The business reasons for adopting an information systems project usually are not disseminated. This is often the case because there are not sound business reasons for adopting such projects, especially those in time-constrained environments. (In Chapter 3 we will argue that business cases are very difficult, because they require estimation of impact that is nearly impossible to accurately estimate.)

3. Accurate project budgets

In rushed projects, budgets may not even be created. Even if they are, it is very common for such budgets to overlook, or grossly underestimate, some key factors. Budgets, however, are important tools for project control.

4. Project support present

Rushed projects never have unqualified support. Some organizational members may continue to oppose such a project long after its adoption by top management. This opposition can manifest itself through open opposition, or simply by small means of uncooperative behavior to delay the project or to reduce its likelihood of succeeding.

5. Project control firmly established

Within organizations, there are always issues concerning control. Good project team unity is the best way to deal with such issues. In rush projects, personnel should be selected considering their ability to work under pressure. In information systems projects involving vendors, related issues often arise. Vendors have their own agenda, with the client organization welfare rarely taking top priority. Control of vendors (and consultants) is key to project success where vendors (or consultants) are present.

6. Rules not changed during project execution

A common feature of project environments, involving specialists assigned on short-term bases, is vanishing resources. Vanishing resources refers to assigned personnel who are often unavailable, especially during key periods. Project manager efforts to complain to the permanent managers of such resources often lead to hostility and greater lack of cooperation. Timely and accurate feedback throughout the project is a way to overcome this potential problem.

Political aspects of information system projects can be very important in project success. This is complicated by the fact that there will always be those who feel that their own interests are furthered by project failure. Human aspects of information systems projects are very complex, and tax the ability of project participants to get along with other people, and to gain progress individually as well as for the benefit of the organization.

Another obvious key need in making a project work is communication. Without clear and accurate communication, project members cannot be expected to know what they are to do, and who to contact for information.

Project Communication

Good communication is a major factor in successful project management. It does not seem to matter whether humans assigned to work on tasks are within the same organization or not, communication barriers naturally arise. In traditional, more permanent organizations, people learn to develop ways to find out what they need to know. Projects are different environments, with high degrees of change and uncertainty. They involve a great deal of change in personnel, along with a dynamic and complex project activity that needs to be accomplished under some time pressure.

Formal project communication devices have been developed. A documented communication plan is an extreme form, and would be appropriate for communicating across organizational lines. This would be appropriate, especially for dealing with vendors and consultants. However, one cannot expect to anticipate every contingency that will arise, and the ability to deal with new situations in a civilized manner is key to long-term relationships needed for organizational success on the part of vendors and consultants.

Simpler project communication techniques have proven effective. In Chapter 1, we discussed the importance of user involvement within projects. A common complaint of system developers is that they get to work only about 20 hours of their normal scheduled week, leading to many night and weekend hours devoted to their projects. One reason is the need for meetings. Successful projects have lots of meetings, both within system development teams and with users. Meetings within development teams are required because there is a need to coordinate activities. Meetings with users are recommended if the support of users upon project completion is expected. Meetings with users are required if the system involves some design uncertainties, and project success depends upon acceptance of the system by the users.

Project Managers

It has been reported that over 30 percent of new software projects are canceled before completion, and that over half are more than 180 percent over budget.[1] A commonly cited reason is poor project planning and management. At the same time, there is a shortage of qualified, large-scale project managers.

Project management involves getting work done through outsiders. We will see in Chapter 3 that projects often involve dual lines of authority. Project managers are not in as powerful a position as managers in other forms of organization, and therefore they have to rely on influence and persuasion to get people to work toward project ends. The survival of a project manager depends a great deal on the strength of the alliances that the manager can make with powerful stakeholders, and by success in competing for resources within the firm. The project manager's mission is to integrate diverse activities in a highly dynamic environment, to produce technical deliverables with a team whose members are temporarily assigned from different parts of the firm and therefore have other loyalties. This must be done within the constraints of a budget for cost and for time, and meeting quality specifications.

The project manager has to make decisions and provide a sense of direction for the project organization, and serve as the hub for project communication. The ability to take on a number of roles is required. The project manager must be an evangelist, to keep everyone believing that the project will work. He or she must also be an entrepreneur, getting the necessary funds, facilities, and people required for project success. The project manager must also be a change agent, orchestrating diverse activities and facilitating these efforts to ensure project success.

The project manager has the responsibility of all managers, to get the job done on time, within budget, and satisfying specifications. The job also includes planning and organizing, dealing with groups representing the owner, and subcontractors. In addition to people skills, the project manager must understand enough technology to realize what is possible and what is not, and to recommend project termination if things are not working out. The project manager needs to be personable, to use a leadership style capable of motivating diverse people who do not work directly for the project manager. The project manager also needs to be able to understand budgeting.

Comparison: Functional and Project Managers

Project managers have to operate in a very turbulent environment. Table 2.2 shows that there are many differences between a project manager's job and that of a functional organization manager.

The selection of a project manager should focus on a number of characteristics. Project managers need flexibility, leadership, confidence, and organizing skills. They should be generalists rather than specialists. They need to communicate well, and to be able to build trust and team spirit. They need general business skills, as well as technical understanding. Project management requires a well-rounded individual.

Team cooperation is critical in projects. Matrix organizations involve high levels of conflict, in large part due to the dual chain of authority found in matrix organizations. Project managers operating in that environment need to function without the authority often found in functional organizations. Within projects, compromise and dealing with conflict in a positive way are usually associated with reduced conflict intensity.

While not always given direct authority, the project manager has control over some resources. The primary source of authority, however, is often the respect gained from professional expertise, and sometimes charm and personality. Professional expertise can be gained from technical knowledge and administrative competence. Some have suggested that project managers try to appear powerful to workers, so that they maximize their influence.

Table 2.2 Comparison of managerial features

Functional Manager	Project Manager

Clear chain of authority
    Quali-permanent
    relationships
    Can direct
	Often operates in matrix structure, with low authority
	Temporary, shared relationships
	Often must motivate positively

Established organization	Developing and changing organization
Long-term relationships	Short-term relationships
Directs a small set of skills	Directs a diverse set of skills

Project managers can be found either inside or outside of the organization. From within the organization, someone with experience and the right specialties is often impossible to find. Therefore, project managers often need to be found from outside the organization. However, this is also problematic, because it takes time to establish alliances, and to learn the organization. But usually people with better organizational skills and experience are available in the broader market outside of the organization.

Summary

Information systems projects are very important, providing valuable computer technology for organizations. There is a wide variety of such projects. Web projects tend to involve many similar projects of a short duration. This makes project management easier than the typical kind of information systems project, which may involve a range of time from a month to years, and tends to involve more variety. The largest scale information systems project is often installation of an ERP system. This third type of project may be quite short if it simply involves adoption of a vendor product. However, it can involve many years for global firms revamping their entire information system support.

Information systems projects have the characteristics of all projects, in that they are first-time endeavors to do something, involving the coordination of people with time a major element. Information systems projects are special in that they usually involve more people focus, and these people bring diverse specialties to the project. There also is often an element of creativity in information systems projects that makes it very difficult to predict how long things are going to take. The waterfall model is often used to describe the activities involved in information systems project, beginning with project proposal and adoption, user requirements analysis, system design, system development, testing, installation, and maintenance.

Human issues are very critical to information system project success. Interpersonal conflict may arise due to individual characteristics, team characteristics, project characteristics, or organizational characteristics.

The role of each of these areas and how problems in each factor can impact projects was reviewed. Successful project completion requires careful management of each of these factors.

The impact of conflict on performance was reviewed. A little conflict is healthy, reducing the likelihood of complacency and urging us to do more and better things. However, conflict can quickly become counter-productive. It is especially difficult to manage conflict in information systems projects, because there are so many diverse people involved, many of them specialists who deal better with computers than with people.

Projects bring together diverse specialists to work on them. This creates a need for effective communication within project teams. IS/IT projects often involve working with outside organizations, such as vendors and consultants. The need to communicate is the same, but crossing organizational lines can impose additional communications barriers. More formal communication can assure better understanding in this case. There also is a need to communicate with the users that are to be the beneficiaries of IS/IT projects. Communication of all three types needs to be frequent to assure shared understanding in the highly dynamic project environment common to IS/IT projects.

The project manager is central to control of the project. The project manager must integrate diverse elements to bring projects in on time, within cost, and with satisfactory performance. The project manager needs to be an individual capable of operating with diverse people, and capable of understanding both technical and administrative aspects of the project.

Information systems project managers are special individuals. They have a daunting task, getting creative work completed in dynamic environments with a great deal of personnel change. Project managers need to deal with top management, business clients as users, and a diverse set of information technology specialists. Information systems project management is a high-pressure job with a great deal of turnover, and the need to coordinate a diverse group with little authority. However, there are very high salaries to compensate.

Recent research on human factors in information systems projects is referenced.[2]

Glossary

Functional manager: Manager of a permanent organization.

Individual characteristics: Result of different personalities, of individuals with different demographic backgrounds as well as education, and experience.

Interdependence: People working together, team effort necessary to make projects work.

Interpersonal conflict: Difficulties encountered by people in getting along with others without friction.

Programmers: Information systems job title responsible to build systems.

Project manager: Individual assigned the responsibility of organizing and managing a project.

Project scope: Statement giving project aims and constraints.

Project team: Group of people charged with accomplishing the project through coordinated efforts of diverse skills.

Systems analysts: Information systems job title responsible for identify system needs and designing the software product.

Waterfall model: Prototypical list of systems development activities usually present in an information systems project.

PMBOK Items Relating to Chapter 2:

1.7 The project manager is the person assigned by the performing organization to lead the team that is responsible for achieving the project objectives.

    1.7.1 Project managers have the responsibility to satisfy task needs, team needs, and individual needs.

    1.7.2 Project managers accomplish work through the project team and other stakeholders.

2.1 An organization's culture, style, and structure influence how its projects are performed.

    2.1.1 Organizations are systematic arrangements of persons and/or departments aimed at accomplishing a purpose, which may involve undertaking projects.

2.1.2 Project management success in an organization is highly dependent on an effective organization communication style, especially in the face of globalization of the project management profession.

2.1.4 Organizational process assets are the plans, processes, policies, procedures, and knowledge bases specific to and used by the performing organization.

10.1 Plan Communications Management—process of developing an appropriate approach and plan for project communications based on stakeholder's information needs and requirement, and available organizational assets.

10.2 Manage Communications—process of creating, collecting, distributing, storing, retrieving, and the ultimate disposition of project information in accordance with the communications management plan.

References

1   See the latest Gartner Group report on the Internet: www.Gartner.com

2   F.T. Jetu and R. Riedl. 2012. "Determinants of Information Systems and Information Technology Project Team Success: A Literature Review and a Conceptual Model," *Communications of the Association for Information Systems* 30, pp. 455–482.

CHAPTER 3

Project Organization

Working on information systems projects will expose you to many forms of organization and to many project managers. This chapter reviews the primary types of organization used for information systems projects, and the reasons they are designed that way. The chapter also discusses features desirable in project managers, critical factors in project success.

The purpose of organization is to coordinate the efforts of many to accomplish goals. Organizational structure shows reporting relationships. Figure 3.1 shows a small subset of reporting relationships in a large organization.

Alternate Organization Structures

Organization structures represent the hierarchical reporting and official communications networks within organizations. The management hierarchy consists of reporting relationships, an official chain of control or authority. This chain of authority deals with official activities, such as hiring, firing, and promotion. It also includes directing the activities of subordinates. Organizations can be grouped into major subdivisions on the basis of a number of frameworks.

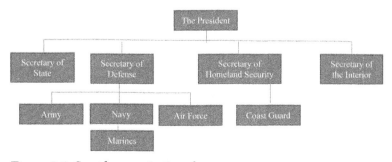

Figure 3.1 Sample organization chart

Informal organization can exist in parallel to the official organization structure. Informal organization consists of the network of personal contacts within the organization, and may consist of cliques and groups of people who work well together, and who may not work well with those outside of their subgroup. In organizations with high levels of professionalism (such as in information systems work), informal networks can be very powerful and positive forces. Informal communication is socially motivated. It is very fast, but is not necessarily thorough or dependable. Project managers, as we shall see, have relatively low levels of official authority.

There are three basic forms of project organization: functional, project, and matrix. Each form of organization has its own benefits, and each works well in certain types of environments. The appropriate organization structure depends on the goal of the organization, the type of work it is supposed to do, and the environment within which it operates.

Functional Organization

Functional differentiation organizes elements by specialization (see Figure 3.2). This form of organization relies more on formal rules, procedures, and coordinated plans and budgets to control operations. In a project context, the project is divided into segments that are assigned to the appropriate functional groups, with each functional group head responsible for his or her segment of the project.

Functional organization works well in repetitive, stable environments. Organizational sub-elements are defined by activity or specialty function. All of the accountants in the firm are collected in one location, where they work together. The same is true for the functions of finance, marketing, and MIS. Operations is a separate function, and operational

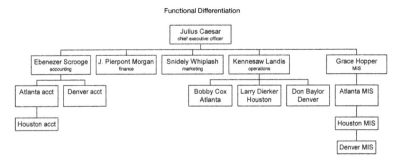

Figure 3.2 *Organizational elements by specialization*

suborganizations are often grouped by geographic location, another optional form of organization. The primary benefit of the functional form of organization is that specialists work together, and can develop professional skills in the most efficient manner. Accountants focus on accounting problems, and become very well trained in accountancy. On the other hand, they gain little exposure to the problems of other organizational elements, such as operations or marketing.

Project Organization

Pure project organization involves creating a separate, independent organization specifically for accomplishing a particular project. One type of example would be the Olympic Committees created to make each Olympic Games work. Once the project is complete, there is no reason for the organization to continue (the next round of games or elections will involve other locations and candidates). Figure 3.3 demonstrates how skills can be grouped by project.

The project center is linked to the parent organization to draw resources and personnel as needed. In the case of Olympic Committees, the permanent International Olympic Committee is available to provide continuity. In the case of committees for elections, there are permanent political parties to draw resources from. Task forces are often announced at a high level, such as the Task Force on Delivery System Reform and Health Information Technology (HITECH) where about $30 billion was invested as part of the Patient Protection and Affordable Care Act. Similar task forces are often created for relocation operations.

Sometimes project organizations are stand-alone organizations. These are newly created organizations for a specific mission, drawn from several

Figure 3.3 Skills grouping

organizations. Examples are large-scale public works, like Hoover Dam, or the Dallas-Fort Worth International Airport. NASA space station development drew people from a number of organizations. Often stand-alone joint ventures are used in the construction business for very large projects beyond the scope of participating firms on their own.

Partial project organizations also exist. In this form, the project manager is responsible for some activities, while other activities that are more support oriented, like accounting, remain with functional divisions. This is a common arrangement.

Matrix Organization

If an organization continually operates in a project mode (many organizations do in construction, in information systems, and in consulting), there is a need to quickly create large project groups. The matrix organization form is a grid-like structure of reporting and authority relationships overlaying traditional functional organization (see Figure 3.4). It is used within organizations that make more than minimal use of project teams or product groups. The improved coordination obtained from project organization is combined with the strengths for each specialty that are provided by functional forms of organization. The matrix form of organization was originally adopted by NASA and by the Department of Defense in the 1960s, when contracting practices required contractors to use project management. For each particular project, the contracting firm had to develop a project organization. PMBOK has unique terminology,

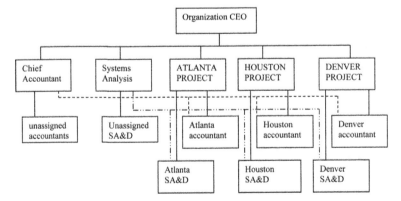

Figure 3.4 Matrix organization

referring to functional matrix organization as a weak matrix and project matrix forms strong matrix. These terms are commonly used by those strong advocates of the Project Management Institute.

The key feature of matrix organization is multiple lines of authority. Specialists report to their functional managers with respect to issues involving their specialty, and report to their project managers for specific assignments. Functional specialists are assigned to the project, usually physically located wherever the project is being implemented. But these specialists depend for their personal career decisions on their permanent functional homes. The project accountant works with the project manager, and the project accountant's job is to keep the project manager informed of the cost performance on the project. Since the accountant will work on a number of projects during his or her career, the project accountant's promotion and raises are often decided by the chief accountant at the accountant's permanent organization. Project managers have some input, but the chief accountant would be the project accountant's permanent supervisor. Once the project was completed, the project accountant would return to the organization's accounting office, where he or she would await the next project assignment, or else undertake professional development such as training, or maybe stay with the accounting office on a permanent basis. The same is true of the project engineer. It could be true for the project manager and production personnel as well, although these people often go into the open market to another organization when the project is completed.

There are some problems introduced by the matrix form of organization. The dual reporting structure creates a state of confusion for those who like high levels of structure. It is said that no man can serve two masters. There also is a military principle of unity of command. The matrix system, with two potential sources of direction, has been found to lead to conflict due to incompatible demands and priorities from two managers of a specific individual. Most people are able to cope with such mixed signals, but it causes distress in others. The ability of managers to compromise, and to deal with conflict, has proven very important in project management. While conflict can sometimes lead to improved performance, it needs to be managed carefully. Matrix forms of organizations call upon managers to do a great deal in a difficult environment.

The level of control used within a project organization should vary with the level of difficulty of the problems expected. If there are major technical issues, stronger centralized organization is merited, with a focus on technical lines of organization. For instance, if a major engineering problem is expected to be critical to the project, engineering components would be centralized under a project engineer. On the other hand, if no major engineering problems were expected, there might not be a project engineer, but rather independent engineers assigned to each work group that needed one. This independence would allow focus on the tasks assigned to the work group rather than overall engineering coordination.

Comparison of Organization Structures in Projects

There are many variations to the three basic organization structures discussed so far in this chapter.

Task Forces

Task forces are temporary groupings of individuals created to solve a particular problem. The task force idea comes from the military, where combining different types of units under a temporary leader for some specific mission is often practiced. In project organizations, individuals with different specialties are grouped together to develop a solution for a specific problem. Long-term task forces can be turned into permanent teams.

Hybrids

Functional matrix and project matrix structures are hybrids of the three basic forms presented above.

A functional matrix organizational structure is used when a project manager is restricted to coordinated functional group assignments. Functional managers are responsible for technical work assignments. The project manager in this case acts as a staff assistant with indirect authority to expedite and monitor project activities.

In a project matrix form of organization, the project manager has more direct authority to decide personnel and work assignments. The functional manager is responsible to provide resources and advisory support to projects.

In the balanced matrix organization, project managers and functional managers have roughly equal authority and responsibility for the project. The project manager typically decides what needs to be accomplished, while the functional managers are responsible for deciding how work will be done and by whom.

Organization Structure for Different Risk Conditions

Projects can involve risks in a variety of forms. Matrix forms of organization were found to be correlated with project success when technical risk was high, because the matrix form of organization had more skilled assets available if needed. When the risk of cost overrun was high, project success was found to be significantly related to understanding of project goals, as well as project manager authority, team support, and communication. Projects that were riskier in terms of budget were found to require more formal planning, monitoring, and control. When schedule risk was high, project success was most correlated with project manager experience, and the level of monitoring.

Projects have three major risk areas—cost, schedule, and technical quality. Risk management of large information systems projects is reported by a GAO study of Defense Department information system projects.[1]

Levels of Project Organization

Projects involve a nontraditional form of organization. Traditional organizational design is much more rigid. While no organization is truly permanent, traditional organizational forms are designed on the assumption that they will continue into the foreseeable future. They are not very flexible, and they react slowly to change.

Projects, on the other hand, are organized with the understanding that they are temporary. Some projects can be very long in duration, such as the construction of a cathedral in the 11th to 14th centuries, taking hundreds of years. Other projects may last only weeks, and therefore have very temporary lives. Projects involve very high levels of uncertainty and change, so project organizations need to be flexible and adaptive.

In the traditional form, people can enhance their professional training and development. Many organizations that contract to undertake projects typically adopt a functional form of organization for permanent assignments, drawing people for individual projects from their permanent assignments to temporarily work with other specialists on specific projects. This is true in construction, engineering, and large accounting firms specializing in consulting, including information system consulting. Careers with such organizations involve a great deal of relocation as individuals leave their home base for the duration of projects to which they are assigned. Between projects, the organizations may value their specialty skills enough to keep them on the payroll. Ultimately, however, new projects are needed in which these skills can be utilized.

Within project organizations, integrators are often used to facilitate communication. **Liaisons** are used to integrate two groups not part of the same organization. Liaisons are especially useful between the people who fund the project and the project team. Project expediters or **coordinators** are individuals whose job is to make sure that something happens. These individuals have no authority, but are assigned to keep on top of problems, so that they can inform project managers of the need for additional resources for specific activities.

Criteria for Selection

Table 3.1 outlines the conditions for which a particular organizational form is most often appropriate.

Other criteria that bear on the project type include uncertainty, cost and time criticality, and the uniqueness of the project. If the project involves high stakes, a matrix form or pure project form gives better control. If there are high levels of certainty, task forces and teams are appropriate

Table 3.1 Comparative organizational forms

Form	Size	Duration	Complexity
Task force	Small to medium	Short to medium	Low to medium
Project team	All	All	Low to medium
Multiple project teams	Medium to large	All	Medium to high
Matrix	Medium to large	All	Medium to high

because they involve less investment. If time and cost are not
forms and teams are also appropriate. If the project is unique
full project form is appropriate.

Summary

Organizational structure is a means to achieve goals and respond to problems. Project personnel are often organized into project teams, or into
a matrix structure. These organizational forms are more flexible than
functional structures, which tend to be more bureaucratic. The positive
and negative features of alternative organizational forms and their vari-
ants need to be understood by top management, so that they can select
the organizational form most suitable for their situation. Understanding
why these forms exist is also important to those working in them. The
matrix form of organization is especially suitable for many projects for
large organizations.

Recent research in information systems project organization is
referenced.[2]

Glossary

Coordinator: see Expediter.

Expediter (or coordinator): Individuals who monitor problems in an
organization and work on alleviating them rapidly.

Functional organization: Organization by type of work group members do.

Hybrid: Mix between functional and matrix organizational forms.

Liaison: Individual integrating two or more groups through personal
communication.

Matrix organization: Grid-like structure of dual reporting relationships
combining functional and project organizational features.

Organization: Structure to coordinate efforts of many to accomplish
shared goals.

Project organization: Organization by project task or groups of tasks.

Task force: Temporary grouping of people of diverse skills with the intent
of accomplishing a specific job.

PMBOK Items Relating to Chapter 3:

1.4.4 A project management office is a management structure that standardizes the project-related governance processes and facilitates the sharing of resources, methodologies, tools, and techniques.

2.1.3 Organizational structure is an enterprise environmental factor, which can affect the availability of resources and influence how projects are conducted.

2.2.2 Project governance is an oversight function that is aligned with the organization's governance model and that encompasses the project life cycle.

2.3.1 The composition of project teams varies based on factors such as organizational culture, scope, and location.

9.1 Plan Human Resource Management—process of identifying and documenting project roles, responsibilities, required skills, reporting relationships, and creating a staffing management plan.

9.2 Acquire Project Team—process of confirming human resource availability and obtaining the team necessary to complete project activities.

9.3 Develop Project Team—process of improving competencies, team member interaction, and overall team environment to enhance project performance.

9.4 Manage Project Team—process of tracking team member performance, providing feedback, resolving issues, and managing changes to optimize project performance.

References

1 C.R. Cha. 2014. *Selected Defense Programs Need to Implement Key Acquisition Practices*.

2 K. Aaltonen. 2011. "Project Stakeholder Analysis as an Environmental Interpretation Process," *International Journal of Project Management* 29, no. 2, pp. 165–183; G.M. Winch. 2014. "Three Domains of Project Organizing," *International Journal of Project Management* 32, no. 5, pp. 721–731.

PART II

Project Adoption and Planning

CHAPTER 4

Project Selection and Approval

The project process begins with a project proposal, generated by users or management. The first step is an initial selection of projects, either on a case-by-case basis, or periodic selection by committees. A related decision of great importance is to keep track of the progress of a project, so that those that are not going to provide value to the organization can be canceled.

Analyzing the expected financial impact of a software project is referred to as a **business case**. Business cases can be accomplished in a number of different ways—some financial, others more subjective; some widely used, some offered as potential improvements. This chapter discusses the decision problem of project selection, and shows how the most commonly used methods work. Analytic methods support this selection process in two ways. First, they provide decision makers with analysis of expected outcomes from adopting specific projects. Second, they provide a basis for communication, so that the reasoning behind a selection decision can be explained to others.

Measurement of Project Impact

Information systems projects typically involve benefits that are difficult to measure in terms of concrete monetary benefits. This vastly complicates sound management, because cost-benefit analysis, the ideal tool for evaluating project proposals, will not always accurately reflect project benefits.

Intangible factors: Both costs and benefits tend to have intangible features. The tangible costs and benefits tend to be historical, backed by data or solid price quotations from vendors. But many of the benefits are expected in the future, and are very difficult to measure. These include expected increases in market share, improved customer service, and better corporate image.

These would all have a significant impact on the corporation's bottom line, but guessing exactly what that impact would be is challenging at best.

Hidden outcomes: Other aspects of information technology projects often involve unexpected results. Information technology projects can impact organizational power. New projects can change the power-specific groups may have held in the past, which can have negative impact on the teamwork of the organization. Information technology also includes components of the organization's communications network. Often different elements of the organization can adopt projects that impact the organizational communications network without this impact being considered. This can result in duplication of efforts, or development of barriers between groups within the organization. Computers can make work more productive and more attractive. But they also can change work roles to emphasize skills in which specific employees have no training, making them feel less productive.

Failure to identify the impact of projects often is not noticed until project implementation. At that stage, the problems created are more difficult to deal with. It is important to consider the systems aspects of projects, and try to predict how the project will change how people do their jobs. Thorough user involvement can make project impact more obvious, as well as easier to reconcile and convince users of the project's benefits.

The changing nature of information technology: There are many excellent applications of computer technology to aid businesses. But a major problem is that technology is highly dynamic. Some information systems projects take years to implement. This can result—and indeed has often resulted—in installation of a new system after it is outdated by even newer technology. McLeod and Smith (1996) suggest a maximum of 9 months between management approval and project component construction in information systems projects.

Selection Practice

Information technology tended to be treated as a capital investment. The following financial techniques have often been used.

1. Payback
2. Discounted cash flow
3. Cost-benefit analysis

Each of these methods will be demonstrated in this chapter. Decision makers treat information technology investment more like operations projects with measurable profitability requirements than the revenue-based appraisals appropriate for training and marketing. Operations investments focus on efficiency-related measures. Conversely, marketing investments are usually viewed in terms of their expected impact on improving competitive position, or increasing market share. The capital approach was found very appropriate for hardware proposals, but difficulties were encountered when justifying software. **Intangible benefits** such as competitive advantage or improved practices tended to be disregarded because they are hard to quantify. The most commonly cited justification was reduction in expenses, usually in payroll. The second most common justification involved the subjective aspect of accomplishing some strategic objective. Intangible benefits cited were enhanced patient care and satisfaction for a health care organization, better speed of responding to customers, and the need to satisfy governmental regulations.

Net present value masks some of the true value of information technology proposals. On the other hand, some projects that have low impact on corporate performance often appear attractive in cost-benefit analyses. This is because cost-benefit analysis emphasizes those features most easily measured. The value of information technology projects is in making organizations more competitive, increasing customer satisfaction, and operating more effectively. These are sometimes the intangible strategic benefits that are often disregarded because they were not measurable.

Information systems projects involve risks from a number of sources. Most of these risks have to do with estimating the time for a specific organization to accomplish required work. The amount of time, on average, will depend on a number of factors, including:

1. Project manager ability
2. Experience with this type of application
3. Experience with the programming environment
4. Experience with the language or system used
5. Familiarity with modern programming practices
6. Availability of critical equipment, software, and programming language
7. Completeness of project team (are all team members on board)

8. Personnel turnover
9. Project team size
10. Relative control of project manager over project team

Of these factors, probably the most important is the ability of the project manager. Experience can take a variety of forms, as indicated by items 2 through 4. Familiarity with modern programming practices concerns exposure to current best practices. These items are a **checklist** of characteristics that should be at minimum acceptable levels. If satisfactory ratings are not assigned for all items, there may be doubt about this organization's ability to complete this particular project.

Cost-benefit analysis should consider costs over the entire life cycle of the project. Simms stated that life cycle costs are roughly four times development costs for most information systems projects. But these long-range costs are much less predictable, and therefore often not included in cost-benefit analyses.

Another issue involves who should do the estimating. In construction, a common practice is to have those who will be responsible for implementing the project do the estimation. This is in a competitive bidding environment, where there is great danger in estimating too low. The motivation is for these estimators to be very cautious. This tends to result in safe estimates considering every possible risk, which is another way of saying that it results in inflated estimates. (Inflating estimates is how you cope with risk at the estimation stage.) In the information systems field, there is far more work to do than capacity to do it. Therefore, the environment is less competitive. While information system consulting is rapidly growing, in the private sector competition is based more on negotiation and perceived quality than competitive bidding on price. Therefore, estimators do not have the motivation to consider all risks. Software developers who estimate their own performance tend to be optimistic.

Reasons for adopting an information technology project include:

- Cost cutting
- Cost avoidance
- Revenue maintenance
- Revenue enhancement

- Entering a new market
- Gaining market share

These include soft benefits that are important, but difficult to accurately quantify, such as developing market share. Those projects that have strategic impact might be recognized as being at a disadvantage when cost-benefit analysis is applied. But strategic projects were critical to business improvements, so they were viewed as necessary investments. Required projects are things that the company has to do to stay in business, such as calculating payroll and complying with regulations. These projects also are adopted. The remainder of the proposed projects are rigorously analyzed for their return on investment using cost-benefit analysis. Projects in this category that fail to meet the firm's return on investment (ROI) standard are held in limbo until better ways of implementing them are found.

Information systems projects involve significant investment on the part of firms. Efficient management of these investments is critical to firm success. However, there is a great deal of difficulty in accurately assessing the costs and benefits involved in most information technology projects. Many companies simply disregard important intangible factors since they involve high levels of uncertainty and even speculation. But there are many important intangible factors involved in assessing the worth of information technology project proposals. Value analysis or multiple criteria analysis offer means of considering such factors.

Project Evaluation Techniques

A number of methods exist to evaluate project proposals, either from the perspective of selecting the best option available, designing an ideal option, or rank-ordering options. This section demonstrates some of the most widely used methods, and shows how other methods can be used to consider other factors describing expected project performance.

General Project Selection

Economic and financial analyses include payback (determining the expected time until investment is recovered) and cost-benefit analysis.

Net present value and internal rate of return extend cost-benefit analysis to consider the time value of money, appropriate when projects are lengthy (three years or more).

Checklists describe criteria of importance and their minimum acceptable levels of requirement. Screening methods are a variant of checklists, eliminating projects that do not have minimum estimated performance on specific measures. Project profiles describe the performance of each project on criteria, so that the decision maker can see each project's strengths and weaknesses. Scoring and rating models are a simple form of multicriteria analysis where measures are obtained on each criterion of importance, and combined in some fashion. Multicriteria decision models are in general more formal than scoring and rating models, but operate on essentially the same principle—identify factors that are important, measure how well each project does on each factor, and combine these into some value score that can be used for ranking.

The rest of this chapter will demonstrate most of the basic methods. The first method demonstrated is screening, a common form of the checklist method that can be and often is combined with other criteria.

Screening

Screening is a process that is very useful in cutting down the dimensions of the decision problem. The way in which screening operates can vary widely in details, but essentially involves identifying those factors that are important, establishing a minimum level of importance, and eliminating those projects that fail on any one of these minimum standards. Obviously, if the standards are set too high, the decision problem disappears as no projects survive the screening. This is appropriate if the minimum standards reflect what management demands in return for their investment.

To demonstrate screening, assume that 100 information systems project proposals are received this month. All of the projects were evidently worthwhile in someone's mind, but management must consider budgets and other resource limitations. Assume that the criteria and minimum performance levels given in Table 4.1 are required:

If any of the 100 proposed projects failed to meet all four of these standards, they would be rejected preemptively. This reduces the number

Table 4.1 Screening example

Expected return on investment	At least 30%
Qualified project team leadership	Available
Company expertise in this type of work	Either company has experience or desires to gain it
Project completion time	Within 48 months

of proposed projects for more detailed analysis. This approach can be implemented by checklists, which give clearly defined standards on those areas of importance to management.

Screening is good at quickly weeding out those projects with unacceptable features. The negative side of screening is that tradeoffs between very good features and these unacceptable features are disregarded. The willingness of decision makers to accept lower ROI for projects with strategic importance is disregarded. For those projects for which such tradeoffs are not important, screening is a very efficient way to reduce the number of proposals to a more manageable number.

In the prior section, we gave a list of risk factors for information system projects. These could be implemented as a **checklist** by management specifying minimum acceptable measures that can be used to screen individual projects. Not all risk elements might apply for a given organization's checklist. An example checklist is given in Table 4.2:

Table 4.2 Example checklist

Factor	**Minimum Standard**
Project manager ability	Qualified manager available
Experience with this type of application	Have experience, or application is a strategically key new technology
Experience with system or language	Personnel with experience can be obtained
Familiarity with modern programming practices	If not, training is available
Availability of critical equipment, software, and programming language	Each critical component available
Project team complete	Key personnel identified and agreed to work; Support personnel easily available

Checklists ensure implementation of policy limits. Checklists are a way to implement screening from the perspective of features management feels are important. The next step in analysis is to more directly compare alternative project proposals.

The intent of a **project profile** is to display how the project proposal compares to standards, as well as how the project compares to other proposals. Profiles have a benefit over screening limits, because poor performance on one factor can be compensated for by strong performance on another factor. For instance, match with company strategic programs can be an important factor. There could be other project proposals that contribute nothing to the firm's strategic program, yet have an outstanding cost improvement for administrative work. This would be reflected in very strong performance on return on investment. Conversely, another project may have a slightly negative return on investment calculation, but may involve entering a new field in which the firm wants to gain experience.

To demonstrate project profiles, assume a firm has a number of information projects proposed. This is generally a large list, because of the many beneficial things information technology can do for organizations. Here we give a short list of six proposals in Table 4.3, measured on resources used, as well as benefits expected.

A profile displays the characteristics of individual projects. Estimated cost is needed to determine if available budget can support a project. The same is true for other scarce resources, such as systems analysts in this case. A tabular form is given above. Graphical displays and ratios are often valuable to give a measure with which relative performance can be measured. For measures such as NPV/Cost ratio, cutoff levels can be used to screen

Table 4.3 Project profiles

Project Identifier	Estimated Cost	Systems Analysts	Cash Flow this Period	NPV/ Cost Ratio	Key to Strategy
A265	230,000	3	100,000	0.43	No
A801	370,000	4	−190,000	0.51	Yes
A921	790,000	5	360,000	0.46	No
B622	480,000	3	−52,000	0.11	Yes
B837	910,000	7	−200,000	0.22	Yes
C219	410,000	3	170,000	0.41	No

out projects. For instance, a 40 percent return on estimated cost in net present terms might be desired. Project B622 and B837 are both below this limit, and might be screened out. However, both of these projects are listed as key to the organization's strategy, and management might be willing to accept lower return for the potential for advancing organizational strategy.

Traditional Analysis

Assume that a company is proposing an information technology project to improve their operations. They can build the system in-house, or out-source (in effect, installing an over-the-counter, or OTC software product). One year has been allocated to develop and install the system (either in-house or OTC). The benefits of the proposed project are expected to be obtained for three years after project completion. Staff will be required to operate the new system. There is some money budgeted to train this staff in the initial year. Staff payroll expenses for this operation include inflation reflected in operating expenses. The company has a marginal value of capital of 15 percent per year.

Cost-Benefit Analysis

The cost-benefit calculation for a new project requires identification of benefits in monetary units. Use of net present value requires identification of the timing of monetary exchanges. The benefit from the new project consists of lowered personnel costs. Calculation of costs and benefits are given in Table 4.4:

The outsourced project appears to have a strong advantage in this case. The cost-benefit ratio requires some convention to describe just what costs are assigned to investment and which to benefits. Operating expenses seem more appropriately combined with savings, but note that different views might yield opposing conclusions.

Ratio: The nominal cost-benefit ratio (disregarding the time value of money) for the in-house project is $365,000/$300,000 = 1.22. This indicates that the project is worthwhile, in that the extra initial expenses of $300,000 would be exceeded by expected benefits by 22 percent. For the outsourced project, this ratio is $780,000/$500,000 = 1.56. By these

Table 4.4 Simple cost-benefit calculation

Year	DEVELOP IN-HOUSE	Operating Cost	Benefit	Net
0	$300,000	$80,000		($380,000)
1		$180,000	$250,000	$70,000
2		$200,000	$350,000	$150,000
3		$225,000	$450,000	$225,000
TOTALS	$300,000	$685,000	$1,050,000	$65,000
Year	OUTSOURCE	Operating Cost	Benefit	Net
0	$500,000	$20,000		($520,000)
1		$60,000	$250,000	$190,000
2		$80,000	$350,000	$270,000
3		$110,000	$450,000	$340,000
TOTALS	$500,000	$270,000	$1,050,000	$280,000

measures, the outsourced project appears to have a significant cost-benefit advantage.

Return on investment (ROI) is defined as net project benefits divided by investment (times 100 if you want to view ROI in percentage return). It can be applied to non-discounted cash flows as with cost-benefit analysis. For long-term projects, discounted ROI should be used, which we will demonstrate in the net present value section.

Cost-benefit analysis should consider costs over the entire life cycle of the project. Life cycle costs are roughly four times development costs for most information systems projects, but these long-range costs are much less predictable, and therefore often not included in cost-benefit analyses.

Payback

Payback is a rough estimate of the time required to recover investment. While simple, payback presents a view of the transaction that is very understandable and important to managers. One alternative may be superior to another on the net present value of the total life cycle of the project. However, cost-benefit analysis does not consider the impact of negative cash flow in early periods. For instance, in our process reengineering

Table 4.5 Payback

Year	In-house Net	Cumulative	Outsource Net	Cumulative
0	($380,000)	($380,000)	($520,000)	($520,000)
1	$70,000	($310,000)	$190,000	($330,000)
2	$150,000	($160,000)	$270,000	($60,000)
3	$225,000	$65,000	$340,000	$280,000

example, the cash flow would be as given in Table 4.5. The Net Benefit column is calculated by subtracting the cost of the new system from the cost of the old system by year. In the first year, this is negative, due to the high investment cost of the new system. In years 2 through 6, the new system provides a positive net benefit relative to the old system.

Both alternatives gain a nominal advantage by the end of year 3 (payback is about 2.7 years for the in-house alternative, about 2.2 years for the outsourced alternative). However, $380,000 has been sacrificed at the beginning for the in-house alternative and $520,000 for the outsourced alternative. One of the most common reasons for company failure in the United States is lack of cash flow. In this case, if the firm has cash-flow difficulties, the outsourced option would be less attractive than if they had adequate cash reserves.

Net Present Value

We can modify the cost-benefit ratio by considering the **time value of money**. In this project, for instance, the nominal expected gains of $1,050,000 are spread out over three years, while the development costs are incurred at the beginning. Having the $380,000 (or $520,000 for the outsourced alternative) would mean that the company would not be able to adopt some other investments (and maybe even force the firm to borrow money). The marginal value of money for the firm is 15 percent per year. **Net present value** converts a time stream of money back to its worth in today's terms (or in terms of the project's start, or any other specific time of reference).

Table 4.6 shows the changes in cash flow between the two systems (shown in the net difference column). Discounting each year's net change in cash flow by the discount rate of 1.15 per year to the t-th power, where

Table 4.6 Net present value

Year (t)	In-house Net	Divide by 1.15^t	Outsource Net	Divide by 1.15^t
0	($380,000)	($380,000)	($520,000)	($520,000)
1	$70,000	$60,870	$190,000	$165,217
2	$150,000	$113,422	$270,000	$204,159
3	$225,000	$147,941	$340,000	$223,556
NPV		($57,768)		$72,932

t is the time period, we get the following. Note that initial expenses are treated as occurring during year 1.

Viewed in this light, relative to obtaining a return of 15 percent per year on alternative investments, adopting the in-house alternative would be like writing a check initially for over $57,000, while the outsourced alternative would be equivalent to a gain of over $72,000.

A related concept is **internal rate of return** (IRR), which is the marginal value of capital for which the net present value of a stream of cash flow would break even, or equal zero. Note that IRR can equate to ROI in that ROI is viewed with discounted cash flow. In this case, the IRR amounts to 1.07 for the in-house alternative, for 7 percent average return, while the IRR of the outsourced alternative is 1.225, or an average return of 22.5 percent. By these measures, the outsourced alternative is attractive and the in-house alternative is not.

Cost-benefit analysis seeks to identify accurate measures of benefits and costs in monetary terms, and uses the ratio benefits/costs (the term benefit-cost ratio seems more appropriate, and is sometimes used, but most people refer to cost-benefit analysis). For projects involving long time frames, considering the net present value of benefits and costs is important.

Other Factors

There are a number of complications that can be brought into the calculation of cost-benefit ratios. One of the most obvious limitations of the method is that benefits, and even costs, can involve high levels of uncertainty. The element of chance can be included in cost-benefit calculations by using expected values. For instance, the demand for production output appears to be increasing. Therefore, using an expected demand of 30,000 units per year is probably conservative. Demand could very well continue to increase. The expected value calculation can be quite complicated in its purest form, consisting of identifying all possible demands for a given year and associating accurate probabilities to each outcome. Instead of getting involved in such a speculative and detailed exercise, most managers do what we did—assume a conservative value. However, it should be recognized that there is added benefit to the new machine in its ability to expand. If this expansion capacity is not considered in the cost-benefit calculation, the new machine option is not accurately evaluated.

For instance, if growth in demand was expected to increase at the rate of 1,000 units per year, this form of benefit for the new machine could be reflected as follows, where an extra ($2 − $1.20) × 1,000 units/year = +$800 in gain is obtained each year. As before, net difference is calculated as the new machine cash flow minus the old machine cash flow. Table 4.7 shows calculations:

Table 4.7 Net present value calculation

Year (t)	Old Machine	New Machine	Net Difference	Divide by 1.15^t
0	0	−$100,000	−$100,000	−$100,000
1	$6,000	$24,000	+$18,000	+$15,652
2	$6,000	$24,800	+$18,800	+$14,216
3	$6,000	$25,600	+$19,600	+$12,887
4	$6,000	$26,400	+$20,400	+$11,664
5	$6,000	$27,200	+$21,200	+$10,540
6	$6,000	$28,000	+$22,000	+$9,511
7	$6,000	$28,800	+$22,800	+$8,571
8	$6,000	$29,600	+$23,600	+$7,715
9	$6,000	$30,400	+$24,400	+$6,936
10	$6,000	$31,200	+$25,200	+$6,229
NPV				+$3,921

This would involve a cost-benefit ratio in net present value terms of $103,921/$100,000 = 1.04, and an ROI of 1.160, greater than the company cost-of-capital of 15 percent.

The cost-benefit ratio does not reflect intangible benefits unless they are presented in monetary terms. Cost-benefit analyses have included measurements for intangible items, but they tend to be given lower values because of the uncertainty involved in their estimates. Detailed analyses of the decision maker's willingness to pay for intangible factors have been conducted, but can be time consuming and less than convincing. Governments have encountered some problems in applying cost-benefit analysis to public works, to include (1) evaluating the benefit of recreational facilities and (2) placing a dollar value on human life. When a dam is built, there clearly is benefit obtained from providing many citizens much improved fishing and water sports. (There also is added cost in depriving citizens of the opportunity to view some flooded historical sites.) The approach usually taken has been to place some dollar value on recreation, based on some very insubstantial measures. The evaluation of human life has also been tackled by economists, who have applied things like the net present value of the expected earnings of those whose lives are expected to be lost in some proposed investment project. This of course involves high levels of speculation as well, because the calculation assumes certain ages, assumes that the only value of a human is what they earn, and disregards who pays and who benefits.

If a firm was threatened with a severe monetary penalty for not complying with a governmental regulation with respect to environmental pollution or safe working conditions, a net present value analysis might well lead to the conclusion that it would be rational to pay the penalty and avoid improving operations. For instance, assume that a blast furnace is pouring out black matter at a phenomenal rate that the government finds terribly offensive. Governmental regulations call for a penalty of $10,000,000 if the pollution source is not cleaned up within one year. Hard-core cost-benefit analysis would identify the cost of cleaning up the facility, which might involve an expense of $12,000,000 in equipment and installation, and an added cost of operations of $5,000,000 per year over the next eight years, the remaining life of the equipment. At a discount rate of 12 percent per year, the net present value of benefits

Table 4.8 Net present value calculation

Year	Benefit	Net	Costs	Net
1	$10,000,000	$8,928,571	$17,000,000	$15,178,571
2	–		$5,000,000	$3,985,969
3	–		$5,000,000	$3,558,901
4	–		$5,000,000	$3,177,590
5	–		$5,000,000	$2,837,134
6	–		$5,000,000	$2,533,156
7	–		$5,000,000	$2,261,746
8	–		$5,000,000	$2,019,416
Total		$8,928,571		$35,552,483

and costs would be as shown below. The Net column shows discounted values for Benefits and Costs. Totals are given at the bottom of Table 4.8:

Here the ratio of net present benefits to net present costs is $8,928,571/$35,552,483 = 0.25, well below 1.0, indicating that the rational decision maker would pay the fine and keep operating as is. But the government did not impose the fine limit for the purpose of raising money. They imposed the fine as a means to coerce polluters to clean up operations. The U.S. Congress has no trouble adding extra zeroes to penalties. If the firm continued to pollute, it is not too hard to imagine the penalty being raised in the future to some much larger figure. There have been actual cases similar to this scenario, where within three years the penalty was raised to much larger values, providing a much different cost-benefit ratio. Benefits are often difficult to forecast.

To demonstrate intangible benefits in our machine investment case, one of the clear advantages the new system has is in its higher level of quality output. The loss of discarded products is included in the analysis. But poor production quality results in more than just identification of products not passing testing limits and rejecting them. Quality comes on a continuous scale. The older machine will in all likelihood include production of a number of products that barely pass test limits, and do not contain desired levels of quality. The customer will accept them, but slowly over time a reputation for inferior workmanship will result. The new machine should improve the company's image with respect to quality. Placing a dollar value on image is pure speculation. Rigorous proponents of cost-benefit analysis would disregard such benefits that are immeasurable as "soft," and not worthy of hard-core analysis. Managers with more vision would recognize that there was a relative advantage for the new machine that was not reflected in the cost-benefit analysis.

An additional benefit of the new machine is that it is more flexible. It has the capacity to respond to larger markets because it has added capacity. At the moment of analysis, there is just the one customer. We have just considered the impact of increased demand on the part of this customer, but there might be additional sources of sales in the future. This again would be highly speculative. A hard approach would require the decision maker to identify a specific expected increase in demand. A soft approach would list flexibility as a measure of importance. There could also be other advantages that are intangible, such as safety of workers, impact on market share, or replenishing capital equipment, so that old facilities do not fall apart, disrupting the ability of the firm to conduct business.

Multiple Objectives

Profit has long been viewed as the determining objective of a business. However, as society becomes more complex, and as the competitive environment develops, businesses are finding that they need to consider multiple objectives. Although short-run profit remains important, long-run factors such as market maintenance, product quality, and development of productive capacity often conflict with measurable short-run profit.

Conflicts

Conflicts are inherent in most interesting decisions. In business, **Profit** is a valuable concentration point for many decision makers because it has the apparent advantage of providing a measure of worth. Minimizing **risk** becomes a second dimension for decision making. There are cash flow needs, which become important in some circumstances. Businesses need **developed markets** to survive. The impact of advertising expenditure is often very difficult to forecast. Yet decision makers must consider advertising impact. **Capital replenishment** is another decision factor which requires consideration of tradeoffs. The greatest short-run profit will normally be obtained by delaying reinvestment in capital equipment. Many U.S. companies have been known to cut back capital investment in order to appear reasonably profitable to investors. **Labor** policies can also have impact upon long-range profit. In the short run, profit will generally be improved by holding the line on wage rates, and risking a high labor turnover. There are costs which are not obvious, however, in such a policy. First, there is training expense involved with a high turnover environment. The experience of the members of an organization can be one of its most valuable assets. Second, it is difficult for employees to maintain a positive attitude when their experience is that short-run profit is always placed ahead of employee welfare. And innovative ideas are probably best found from those people who are involved with the grass roots of an organization—the workforce.

This variety of objectives presents decision makers with the need to balance conflicting objectives. We will present the simple multi-attribute rating technique (SMART), an easy to use method to aid selection decisions with multiple objectives.

The **simple multi-attribute rating theory (SMART)** method offers a simple way to quantify subjective elements. There are two elements to the value function in SMART: factor weight (w_i) and score (s_{ij}) of each alternative j on each factor. Overall value is then:

$$value_j = \sum_{i=1}^{k} W_i \times S_{ij}$$

Weights w_i can be obtained in a number of ways, but a simple estimate with some reliability involves ranking the factors, considering the range of likely performances, and then estimating the relative value of moving from the worst to the best performance relative to such a swing from either the most important or the least important. We will do both, and use a rough average of these two estimates. In the example used earlier in this paper, assume that the ranges and rankings for the five criteria are as given in Table 4.9.

First, the extreme expected measures for each criterion are identified, in order for the decision maker to understand the range of possibilities to compare. Then, the decision maker ranks the importance of swinging from the worst measure to the best measure for each criterion. In this case, the

Table 4.9 Criteria weight development

Criterion	Worst	Best	Rank	Best = 100	Worst = 10
Risk	Very high	Very low	2	70	120
Market share	Very negative	Very positive	1	100	150
Control	Low	High	5	5	10
Investment	$1,000,000	$100,000	4	25	40
Return (NPV)	0%	100%	3	50	80

decision maker considered it most important to move market share impact from very negative to very positive, followed by moving risk from very high to very low, moving expected return from 0 percent to 100 percent, investment from $1 million to $100,000, and finally (and least important) moving control from low to high. Next the decision maker is asked to quantify these changes. Viewed from the perspective of the most important criterion, if changing market share impact from very negative to very positive were worth 100, the decision maker assigned a value of 70 to risk, 50 to return, 25 to investment, and 5 to control. To get a second estimate, with 10 assigned to the least important criterion (control), the assigned values were 40 for investment, 80 for return, 120 for risk, and 150 for market share. This information is then used to generate the set of weights w_i. Each of the sets of assigned weights is totaled, and each entry divided by the appropriate total. This gives two estimates of weights, which the decision maker can use to compromise (preferably using rounded numbers) as in Table 4.10.

The scores (s_{ij}) for each alternative on each criterion are now needed. These can be assigned directly, to reflect any kind of utility function for each criterion. Better performance should always receive a higher score than an inferior measure. A possible set of assigned scores are given in Table 4.11.

Table 4.10 SMART calculation of weights

Criterion	Best = 100	Divide by sum	Worst = 10	Divide by sum	Compromise
Risk	70	0.28	120	0.30	0.29
Market share	100	0.40	150	0.375	0.39
Control	5	0.02	10	0.025	0.02
Investment	25	0.10	40	0.10	0.10
Return (NPV)	50	0.20	80	0.20	0.20

Table 4.11 SMART value calculation

Weights	0.29	0.39	0.02	0.10	0.20	1.00
Criteria	Risk	Mkt Share	Control	Invest	NPV	Values
In-house	0.1	0.5	0.9	0.8	0.1	0.342
Outsource	0.8	1.0	0.3	0.6	0.9	0.868

In this case, the outsourced alternative has a clear advantage.

Summary

We have reviewed some of the primary methods used to evaluate project proposals. Screening provides a way to simplify the decision problem by focusing on those projects that are acceptable on all measures. Profiles provide information that display tradeoffs on different measures of importance. Cost-benefit analysis (with net present value used if the time dimension is present) is the ideal approach from the theoretical perspective, but has a number of limitations. It is very difficult to measure benefits, and also difficult to measure some aspects of costs accurately. One view of dealing with this problem is to measure more accurately. Economists have developed ways to estimate the value of a life, and the value of scenic beauty. However, these measures are difficult to sell to everybody.

A more common view is that it is wasted effort to spend inordinate time seeking a highly unstable and inaccurate dollar estimate for many intangible factors. Value analysis is one such alternative method. Value analysis isolates intangible benefits from those benefits and costs that are more accurately measurable in monetary terms, and relies upon decision maker judgment to come to a more informed decision. The SMART method, one of a family of multiple criteria decision analysis techniques, provides a way to quantify these intangible factors to allow decision makers to tradeoff values.

Cost-benefit provides an ideal way to proceed if there are no intangible factors (or at least no important intangible factors). However, usually such factors are present. Intermediate approaches, such as payback analysis and value analysis, exist to deal with some cases. More complex cases are better supported by multiple criteria analysis. In cases of constraints, such as budgets, it is sometimes appropriate to optimize over some objective. Linear programming provides a means of generating the best portfolio of funded projects subject to constraint limits given that accurate measures of project performance are available.

Recent research in information systems project selection is referenced.[1]

Glossary

Business case: Financial analysis of a proposed information systems software project.

Checklist: A means of evaluating initial project proposals in terms of a list of expected characteristics.

Cost-benefit analysis: Economic analysis pricing all factors, dividing benefits by investment.

Discounted cash flow: Conversion of cash flows into their worth as of some base period, usually the present.

Intangible factors: Items of value that are difficult to quantify in monetary terms.

Internal rate of return: The marginal value of capital that yields a net present value of zero for a stream of cash flow.

Multiple criteria analysis: Analysis considering not only one measure of value (such as profit), but the value tradeoffs over multiple measurement scales.

Net present value: The worth, in today's terms, of a stream of cash flow over time, assuming a given marginal cost-of-capital.

Optimization models: Models of decisions allowing identification of the decision that is optimal with respect to selected criterion (or criteria).

Payback: Financial analysis estimating the time required to recover investment.

Project profile: A display of expected project performance on important criteria, allowing comparison of alternative projects.

Return on investment (ROI): Rate of financial return on investment, defined as net profit divided by investment.

Screening: A method of implementing a checklist for project evaluation by listing the worst acceptable performance on a list of criteria.

SMART: Simple multi-attribute rating theory, a means of objectively comparing the values of projects considering multiple criteria.

Tangible benefits: Benefits that are measureable; in cost-benefit terms, measurable specifically in monetary terms.

Time value of money: The current worth of future flows of cash.

PMBOK Items Relating to Chapter 4:

1.6   Business value is defined as the entire value of the business.

   2.4.1   All projects can be mapped to the generic project life cycle structure of start, organize and prepare, carry out, and close.

   2.4.2   A project phase is a collection of logically related project activities that culminates in the completion of one or more deliverables.

7.1   Plan Cost Management—process that establishes the policies; procedures; and documentation for planning, managing, expending, and controlling project costs.

12.1   Plan Procurement Management—process of documenting project procurement decisions, specifying the approach, and identifying potential sellers.

12.2   Conduct Procurements—process of obtaining seller responses, selecting a seller, and awarding a contract.

References

1   A.H. Ghapanchi, M. Tavana, M.H. Khakbaz, and G. Low. 2012. "A Methodology for Selecting Portfolios of Projects with Interactions and under Uncertainty," *International Journal of Project Management* 30, no. 7, pp. 791–803.

CHAPTER 5

System Development

There are seemingly unlimited proposals for implementation of computer systems to aid organizations. Every time one of these proposals is adopted, it creates the need for an information systems project—to bring an application online. Project management is one of the most important developing areas in information systems. It is difficult to bring an information systems project to completion on time, within budget, and meeting specifications. There are many citations of the scope of this problem. A partner of KPMG Peat Marwick said that, on the basis of a survey of 250 companies, some 30 percent of information systems projects exceeded the original budget and time frame by at least a factor of 2, or did not conform to specifications. A report issued by The Standish Group reports industry statistics every year, but these statistics are very stable. Only around 15 percent come in on time and within budget. For large companies, the success rate is closer to 10 percent. It was also reported that only about 40 percent of planned features and functions end up in the final version of the software. Over half of the software development projects initiated by large companies cost nearly 200 percent more than originally estimated. Yet information systems projects offer great value for companies.

In order to develop systems efficiently, a methodology needs to be applied. Organizations use a wide variety of methodologies. The purpose of this chapter is to provide an overview of traditional systems development methodologies. It is becoming more and more important to apply continuous improvement standards to the processes used within business. Standards such as ISO 12207 (disseminated originally in 2008) and Software Engineering Institute's Capability Maturity Model focus on improving the processes of software development. Software development organizations are being required by some user organizations to certify compliance with these standards. Compliance is also very beneficial to software-producing organizations. We will review these standards. Types of information systems projects and their features are examined, followed by a broad framework of the systems development approach.

Requirements analysis identifies the data and information needed to automate some organizational task and to support achievement of organizational objectives. Many information systems failures have been attributed to a lack of clear and specific information system requirements. Accurate identification of requirements early in the process has been reported to lead to more successful systems, and lower costs for error correction.

Requirements analysis can consist of four processes:

- conceptual design
- logical design
- validation
- formal specification

Conceptual design is the process of developing a model of what the system should do. Critical factors such as the implementation environment, organization goals and policies, product and service flows, and anticipated problems need to be identified.

The **logical design** process is where strengths and weaknesses of the conceptual design are assessed. Organizational and technological factors both have to be considered. Organizational factors include resources required, organizational politics, and priorities. Organizational factors are better understood by viewing projects as systems collecting interacting components with a common purpose. Technological factors refer to existing systems capabilities, the availability of needed data, and the availability of needed personnel. The logical design process is a system design considering the organization's strengths and weaknesses.

Validation is a process meant to ensure that a valid set of requirements has been developed. Features that need to be considered in the validation process include data entry methods, system outputs, and other impacts of the proposed project on the overall system.

The **formal specification** is the result of requirements analysis. The statement of work and business case can be used to document the project in terms of its intended mission. An ideal formal specification clearly specifies a complete set of information requirements, to include inputs and outputs, and what these elements are to do.

This process then culminates in the project sponsors creating a project **charter**, a formal authorization for work to proceed. The formal specification focuses on project technical matters. The project charter can be used for the organizational budgetary process to enable activity to proceed within proper control of authorized stakeholders. The charter includes a detailed description of the project in the form of project **scope**, which defines what will be included in the project.

Overview of Analysis and Design Methods

There are a number of approaches that traditionally have been used to analyze and design information systems projects. The laissez faire "code-and-fix" model, where code is written and problems are fixed, resulted in many problems when it came to implementation, and fixing was often expensive.

The Waterfall Model

The waterfall model recognizes feedback loops between stages of software development stages to minimize rework, as well as incorporating prototyping as a means to more thoroughly understand new applications. The waterfall model (named because each step follows its predecessor in sequence) consists of the following stages, each of which can involve reversion to the prior stage if attempts at validation uncover problems. The waterfall model (Table 5.1) has the advantages of encouraging planning before design, and decomposes system development into sub-goals with milestones corresponding to completion of intermediate products. This allows project managers to more accurately track project progress, and provides project structure.

The list shown is for a software life cycle product. Variations in the stage labels are used for different types of project, such as acquisition of software, implementation of a vendor system, or other kinds of projects. Each stage involves a test, either validation or verification. Validation is the process of evaluating software to ensure compliance with specification requirements.

Table 5.1 The waterfall model of software life cycle stages

Stage	Feedback determinant
System feasibility	Validation
Software plans and requirements	Validation
Product design	Verification
Detailed design	Verification
Code	Unit test
Integration	Product verification
Implementation	System test
Operations and maintenance	Revalidation

(Is this the right product?) Verification is the process of determining whether or not the software component functions correctly. (Is the product built right?)

In the original waterfall model, problems accumulated over stages and were not noticed until project completion, resulting in very expensive code. User needs were often not met, resulting in rejection of products after they were built. Therefore, feedback loops were added, along with prototyping to catch problems early. The waterfall model does not allow rapid response to the pervasiveness of change in information system projects. The orderly sequence of activities in the waterfall model does not accommodate new developments. Some systems, especially those involving higher levels of uncertainty and with less investment at stake, are often designed and built using more flexible development methods, such as rapid prototyping, object-oriented process, or rapid application development.

Prototyping is the process of developing a small working model of a program component or system with the intent of seeing what it can do. Thus, it is a learning device, appropriate especially when users are not absolutely sure what they want in a system. Prototyping can be a valuable part of the waterfall approach.

Prototyping

When dealing with systems, which involve beneficial features that are difficult to both predict and price, the systems development approach has proven ineffective. What happens is that the hard, clear dollar benefits rarely are sufficient to justify adopting the system.

A prototyping approach involves building a small-scale mock-up system, allowing the user to try it out. The user could then ask for modifications based upon a better idea of what the system could do. Prototyping is a much less thoroughly planned approach, but is often appropriate for applications with low investment and low structure. This can result in much lower development cost and time, especially when there are many uncertainties about what the system should consist of.

Prototyping is very useful in leading to greater understanding in project requirements definition. It also has been found to improve design effectiveness, because users are directly integrated into the design process in a manner that they clearly understand. Prototyping is not appropriate for all types of system development. However, for smaller scale systems, prototyping is a very effective means of demonstrating what proposed systems would be able to do.

Agile Software Development

A response to the poor performance record of information systems with respect to time, budget, and functionality, some in the software industry have developed collaborative techniques to develop software much faster and closer to user requirements. These techniques are known as agile methods, and include a number of versions. However, the common bases for these techniques include working closely with users throughout the project, iteratively develop software versions in the spirit of prototyping, demonstrating these prototypes with users to identify required changes in direction, and avoiding heavy documentation in favor of getting software developed faster.

Agile methods have proven very effective when applied to small projects. They also work (with care) for larger projects, although effort is needed to get teams to work well together. The best case is when a small, self-organized and motivated team located in the same location work with a small number of on-site customers. There are even cases when teams have worked in a geographically separated environment, although synchronization of efforts is required.

The economy in recent years has had a major impact of the software industry. Because of the increased importance of bringing software products to market faster, revision of traditional methods has been apparent. Agile methods are techniques of software development designed to deliver these products faster, with more functionality necessary to users.

There are many different techniques that have been used in this effort to attain agile programming. These include collaborative techniques (pair programming, having customers work on-site as team members). What this amounts to is a much closer working with customers to ensure that the software products developed are what customers needed. For instance, a common agile practice is to have customers write acceptance tests. This approach emphasizes:

- Focus on individuals and their interactions over focus on processes and tools.
- Delivering working software is more important than comprehensive documentation.
- Customer collaboration is sought rather than contract negotiation.
- Response to change is preferred to following plans.

The agile approach maximizes cooperation with users that has been found to be so critical to information system project success. The principles behind the agile movement are:

- Highest priority is given to satisfy the customer through early and continuous delivery of valuable software.
- Requirements changes are welcomed, even late in the development process. Agile processes harness change with the aim of improving customer competitive advantage.
- Working software is delivered frequently, from a couple of weeks to a couple of months, preferably shorter timescales.
- Cooperative work between business people and developers is needed on a daily basis.
- Projects are built around motivated individuals, who operate in a positive environment with all the support they need, and who are trusted to get the job done.
- Face-to-face conversation is relied upon as the most efficient and effective method of communication.
- The primary measure of progress is working software.

- Agile processes promote sustainable development.
- Technical excellence and good design are sought continuously, enhancing agility.
- Simplicity is essential, seeking to maximize the amount of work not done.
- Self-organizing teams develop the best architectures, requirements, and designs.
- Teams reflect on ways to become more effective at regular intervals, and tune and adjust behavior accordingly.

The agile approach is often combined with other methodologies in hybrid forms.

Other Options for Systems Development

Many projects are developed from scratch, applying conventional systems development approaches. The following iterative life cycle approaches where tasks are performed repetitively to more exactly meet their goals.

- **Component Assembly Projects**: typically object-oriented modules for use in a variety of other applications
- **Rapid Application Development**: techniques to compress the life cycle, to include computer aided software engineering (CASE) and Joint Application Development (JAD). CASE tools involve a degree of reuse of previously developed systems. In order to complete projects on an accelerated timescale, project objectives and scope need to be identified early, and joint development of user requirements must be effective. Group systems, as discussed in Chapter 3, may be of use in this type of application. Care must be taken in assigning team members on a full-time basis, and heavy user participation is very important. Rapid application development can lead to reduced development time, lower development cost, greater user and employee satisfaction, and lower ultimate maintenance costs. However, it is appropriate for small projects, and not those involving significant levels of complexity.

Software Development Standards

Quality improvement has been an area of major development in the operations management area. One of the key ideas involved is that of continuous improvement—developing a philosophy of business in which the way in which work is done (processes) are continuously reviewed with the intent of improving them. This emphasis on quality process has been widely implemented in the United States in the annual Baldrige Award competition, as well as the European Quality Award Assessment Model. Two other programs which have had a major impact in the software development industry include ISO 9000 (European standards for production and management processes) and the Software Engineering Institute's Capability Maturity Model.

The Software Engineering Institute's **Capability Maturity Model** includes five levels of maturity. These are shown in Table 5.2, along with actions generally required to move from one level to another. Organizations that have done nothing to improve their software development methods are assigned to level (1), and are considered to involve high levels of risk and a focus on survival.

Table 5.2 Capability maturity model features

Level	Features	Key processes
1. Initial	Chaotic	Survival
2. Repeatable	Individual control	Software configuration management Software quality assurance Software subcontract management Software project tracking and oversight Software project planning Requirements management
3. Defined	Institutionalized process	Peer reviews Intergroup coordination Software product engineering Training program Organization process definition Organization process focus
4. Managed	Processes measured	Quality management Process measurement and analysis
5. Optimized	Feedback for improvement	Process change management Technology innovation Defect prevention

Moving from the initial level (1) to level (2) requires instilling basic discipline into people management activities. This is accomplished through adopting software management approaches.

Moving from level (2) to level (3) requires that organizations identify the primary competencies required in processes, and taking action to make sure that the people assigned to these activities have these competencies. This can be done through training or hiring. Processes are defined and institutionalized in level (3) organizations.

Moving from level (3) to level (4) requires quantitative management of organizational growth in human management capabilities, and establishment of competency-based teams. Process measurement and analysis needs to be implemented.

Moving to the last level requires continuous improvement of methods for developing personal and organizational process abilities. In this state, greater technology innovation is expected by some. All expect better defect prevention.

Projects accomplished by organizations at various levels for a typical 500,000 line (500 kLOC) software project have been studied. The results dramatically indicate the benefits of attaining higher levels of capability maturity, shown in Table 5.3:

It is clear that adopting capability maturity principles pays. Level 1 projects are expected to take far longer (thus costing far more). They also have much inferior quality as measured by defects. Implementing the capability maturity model requires significant investment, effort, and discipline. However, it is clearly better than the *ad hoc* state of doing nothing.

Table 5.3 **CMMI (*Capability maturity model integration*) *effectiveness***

Level	Development cost $ million	Development time months	Product quality defects/kLOC	LOC/hr
1	33	40	9	1
2	15	32	3	3
3	7	25	1	5
4	3	19	0.3	8
5	1	16	0.1	12

Information System Project Types

There are a wide variety of possible information system projects. There are three basic types of information system projects: maintenance, conversion, and new systems development.

- Maintenance
- Conversion
- New Systems Development

Another scale, which can overlap the three categories given above, is as follows:

- Systems Architecture Projects: projects that are part of the strategic systems plan for the organization, supporting the firm's business strategy
- End User Computing: installing a system for target users, with heavy user involvement in development
- Business Re-engineering Projects: implementing new ways of processing business functions
- Technology Implementation Projects: installation of technology such as a network or e-mail
- Package Implementation: installing a pre-written application, with any required modifications

Each of these implementation project categories can be found in each of the three categories of maintenance, conversion, and new systems development, although to varying degrees. Systems architecture projects are the focus of the information system, and most maintenance work would be expected in this project category. Business re-engineering can involve maintenance and conversion, but would be expected to involve new work for the most part. Conversion work often arises from corporate takeovers, or when new systems architectures are adopted.

Maintenance

Maintenance projects are by far the most common type of information system project. They can arise from the need to fix errors, to add enhancements to some system, or can involve major enhancements. The way in which maintenance work is treated depends on a great deal on the impact of the system in question to the organization's master plan. If the system being maintained is extremely important, it will NOT be treated as a project. It would have a permanent unit assigned to do whatever needs to be done. Some organizations use maintenance work as a training ground for new employees. This is a good type of work to get exposure to the spectrum of the organization's operations.

Fixing errors involve clear purposes—to make the system work correctly. The complexity of this type of work depends on the nature of the system, the error, and the personnel impacted. The best case is a small system, with easily traced errors. It is also easier if someone who has experience with the system is around to assign to fix it.

Minor enhancements involve things such as adding, modifying, or deleting data or reports from the information system. Sometimes minor enhancements involve a degree of original design work. Usually, however, this type of work is constrained by the original design. Minor enhancements are not typically critical. Therefore, there are likely to be more alternatives that can be considered. Minor enhancements are most likely to be assigned to those with design capabilities and knowledge of the organization.

Major enhancements involve high levels of design and implementation. This type of work can involve wide-scale modification of an existing module, or development of a new module. Sometimes a collection of minor enhancements with some common characteristic are packaged together to make a major enhancement. Major enhancement work calls for experienced personnel.

Major enhancements are easiest if the maintenance personnel know the system well, and involve straightforward processes. It is obviously easier if a CASE tool was used to develop the original system, because it can be used to make the modification as well. Major enhancements are more trouble when new personnel are assigned to accomplish them, when it is hard to assess the criticality of the system, and when there are no design and implementation standards available.

Conversion Projects

Conversion projects involve changing an existing system. This existing system does not necessarily even have to be currently computerized (if you can imagine manual information system components in this day and age, but every system has to start somewhere). Most conversion projects consist of moving an application from one computer platform to another. There also are many projects that develop from firm acquisitions in the form of **legacy** systems. Legacy systems create enormous potential for difficulties in integrating systems based on entirely different platforms.

Converting manual systems is the closest maintenance project to pure design and development. The major problems that one should expect in this type of environment are improper specifications and failure to accommodate changes. In order to successfully do this type of work, one would need to understand the existing system, what is desired, and the means to move from the first state to the second.

Managing conversion change depends a great deal on senior management support. The affected employees need to be informed about the change, and it is a lot easier if they can be convinced that their working environment will be easier after the conversion. Often conversions change what employees do, and some people have problems with that. In extreme cases, conversions may displace employees, because either different skill levels are required after conversion, or possibly jobs are eliminated. In this case, one hopes that the displaced employees can be retrained for other work.

Conversion of new technology is easiest when there is a great deal of similarity between new and old hardware and new and old operating systems. It is also easier if existing applications are modular, and if vendors supply routines for conversion. The worst case is when major changes occur, especially if there is a change from a single task to multitask environment. It is difficult, for instance, to move from a line-oriented system to an icon-oriented system like Windows.

Language-based conversions are often encountered. This involves translation from one language to another, usually from a third-generation language like COBOL to a fourth-generation language. In these situations, it helps a great deal to have experts in both the old and new languages on the project team. It is necessary to consider the impact on data structures and code structure. It is usually wise to take full advantage of the capabilities of the newer language.

Non-procedural conversions have unique characteristics. Instead of a sequential control, statements written in the form of rules are fired when all conditions are satisfied, as in a rule-based expert system. Object-oriented approaches are becoming more common, where objects have the power to control processing. Again, it is good to have expertise in both the old and the new languages. In the case of converting to object-oriented systems, it is possible to take advantage of code reuse.

Hardware conversions can arise from the need to convert to a new platform for marketing purposes, from pulling an outsourced application back in-house, or from purchase of a new computing platform. Most of the effort involved in this type of conversion arises from converting low-level input and output-processing routines.

If hardware is obtained from the same vendor that provided the old system, there are fewer problems. Switching from one vendor to another is obviously much more difficult. The best case is when vendor specific input/output is localized in routines supplied by the vendor. Occasionally, however, some adjustments are required.

New Systems

There are many ways in which technology can be used to enhance the information system flow, as well as accomplish needed work.

New System development involves different management characteristics by type of system. The types of systems we will discuss are:

- Transaction processing
- Management control
- Decision support systems (DSS)
- Data warehousing and data mining
- Group support systems
- Executive information systems
- Enterprise resource planning
- Internet commerce

Transaction processing is generally focused on efficient operation. The application will usually involve high volumes of quantitative data from a variety of input sources. These data are used to generate standard reports as part of the information system. Most of the complexity arises from the volume of computations. Sound systems analysis and design procedures should be followed to thoroughly examine the impacts of the new system on everyone affected.

Management control is more specialized than transaction processing. Example applications are to monitor manpower allocations, progress of project activities, production by unit, and sales by region or sales representative. These systems often compare expected performance with actual performance, and if the difference is great enough, some action may be triggered. Clearly this type of system requires more flexibility. Because multiple numbers of people are affected by changes, systems analysis and design processes should be adopted.

Decision support systems by definition are meant to be customized for the specific user. The application of a DSS is to explore decision alternatives. Often data need to be accessed from a variety of sources, some from internal sources, and sometimes from online commercial sources. Each individual decision maker will have his or her own preferences for data, computer interface, and model access. The project team installing a decision support system must have knowledge of the models to be installed. A complicating factor is that the decision maker may not have much idea of what features are desired until the system is in operation. Therefore, a prototyping approach is usually more appropriate for development of a decision support system.

Data warehousing and **data mining** are new technologies that expand the concepts of database systems and statistics (as well as artificial intelligence). Data warehousing applications allow access of vast quantities of data, including cash register data, which can be searched electronically to gain insights into many marketing and financial environments. Data warehouses provide repositories where large amounts of data can be stored in a manner that allows rapid recovery. Data mining applies electronic technology to try to identify customer clusters that would have a greater payoff in response to marketing campaigns, and other statistical analyses of large data sets. The advent of big data, combined with machine-learning software for analysis, is often referred to as **informatics**.

Enterprise resource planning systems are systems designed to comprehensively serve all computing needs of an organization. These systems are usually implemented in modules, but this type of product usually takes over an organization's computing, as the intent is to integrate systems. Enterprise resource planning systems are not trivial to implement, but vendors are more than willing to provide assistance (at the normal nominal fee).

Implementing **Internet commerce** involves rethinking the businesses and its key processes, developing an appropriate and affordable information technology infrastructure, and constructing specific Internet products and services.

There are many kinds of systems that need to be installed, lending variety to many information systems projects found in business.

Systems Development Approach

The systems development approach provides a rational way to evaluate information systems projects. The systems development approach is based on a complete life cycle analysis. Project proposals evaluated by this approach are measured on cost, time, and performance. **Cost** is concerned with resources being spent as expected. Accurate budgets and benefit estimates are needed to accurately evaluate proposals. They also provide valuable control mechanisms during project implementation. **Time** is a critical variable in projects. First, it is highly correlated with cost. Second, delayed benefits are worth much less than early benefits, due to the time value of money. Keeping a project on schedule is a major challenge. **Performance** is a critical third measure. Projects need to perform to specifications and user requirements.

Later, when the project is being implemented, these measures are critically important. Performance needs to be ensured through quality testing. Time is a major means of evaluating how well the project is progressing. We will later look at Gantt charts as a means of planning the time dimension of projects. Cost budgets are also critically important in controlling project implementation. Because of the high levels of uncertainty inherent in projects, management must closely monitor project progress, and be prepared to shift resources and replan activities as required.

System life cycles consist (in broad terms) of the activities of specification, design, coding, data conversion, testing, and implementation. These activities tend to be serial, although data conversion can proceed in parallel with coding.

Specification

Projects start with somebody's problem. Computer systems are powerful tools that solve many problems. Therefore, there are many times when they offer improved means of doing things.

Once a proposed application is identified, a systems analyst who understands how to build such systems needs to be obtained to plan a solution. The systems analyst needs to start off by talking to the people that proposed the application to find out what they want, and to the people that are budgeting the project to find out the constraints in terms of cost that need to be considered. It is best to discuss the proposed project with all groups affected, so that something is not designed that will be counterproductive or create unexpected problems. After these interviews, a clearer statement of the problem should be developed. An effective way to proceed is to identify alternate solutions, and to determine the costs and expected performance features of each, so that the budgeting authority can select the best system possible. A **feasibility study** is a clear, concise statement of the problem, followed by a detailed formal description of the current system describing the problem. Adequate qualitative and quantitative information should be provided to determine whether the effort should be continued. The elements and components of the proposed system are identified.

The specification phase should provide a clear problem statement of what the system is intended to do, with a rudimentary idea of a systems solution. Once the initial authorization is obtained, the system is defined in greater detail. A **statement of work** specifies what is to be done. This needs to specify new system objectives, and provide measures for the acceptability of the system upon completion. Performance objectives should not be constrained by the existing system. One approach that works well is to start with general objectives. Objectives should include sub-elements that are measurable. This phase of the systems development approach results in a comprehensive list of activities, along with their schedules, costs, and required resources. This includes hardware and software requirements. When presented with the costs of proposed systems, many are rejected. It is in the specification phase that most projects die.

Design

The design phase develops how software will meet requirements. One of the classic business analyses is the decision to **make or buy**. This decision is very pertinent to computer systems, because there are many vendors that produce and sell many useful computer systems. Every organization has the option of buying products from vendors, or of building the product themselves. In general, buying products from vendors is much less hassle. But you have to live with the features that the vendors put into the product. They make a living telling everyone that this is exactly what they need. In truth, it often isn't. Furthermore, even if it is, vendors may charge more than the product is worth. But building products in-house requires a lot more risk and time. If required expertise is not available, it may well be worth spending a little more on the vendor. Usually the vendor route is faster, and quite often it is cheaper. The problem usually lies with matching the existing system, and doing the job required.

Recently, it has become very popular to hire out large portions of information processing, or **outsourcing**. One purpose of outsourcing is downsizing. Many functions can be outsourced, including data center management, telecommunications, disaster recovery, and legacy systems maintenance. This avoids the need to waste scarce resources, and can gain efficiencies by hiring vendors with expertise. Outsourcing can also be used for company Internet operations. If plans are clearer, Internet functions that could be outsourced include connectivity, Web server hosting, firewall security, Web site development, and content development. These activities are complex, subject to change, and not particularly relevant to organizational core competencies. Outsourcing makes sense when fast start-up is important, internal skills are lacking, and the vendor can provide strong features. Outsourcing for Internet operations is not as worthwhile if they are of strategic importance to the business, or requirements are ill-defined. Rarely is outsourcing used for everything involved within a project. For one thing, there will be need for internal training to implement the system, and to integrate it with the existing system.

If vendors or outside contractors are being considered, a **request for proposal** is required including the feasibility study and the plan for project development. The request for proposal states the user requirements in terms of system objectives, project scope, and performance specifications as well as constraints, especially in terms of time. It is necessary to develop a qualified bidders list of those with the ability to accomplish the work required.

The project team needs to be selected at this stage. The project manager should be selected, with characteristics we will discuss later. Team members are drawn from functional areas. Functional managers should be sold on the project, so that good team members are obtained.

The output of the design stage is a detailed list of user requirements and system requirements. Tasks are broken down into work packages, and team members are given specific assignments. The project manager is responsible to set up schedules, budgets, and controls. The output of the design stage is a task breakout, with each task scheduled by date. It is necessary to continue close coordination between the systems analyst, the ultimate user of the system, and the budget authority. A project never is completely designed, nor finally adopted, until it is complete. The more accurate the understanding between the analyst, user, and owner is necessary to develop systems that are useful and cost effective.

Code (or Acquisition)

Options, in-house or vendor, need to be evaluated. If in-house, the conventional phase of coding to implement the design is applied. If options including purchasing the products or services of a vendor are adopted, the term acquisition seems more appropriate. Whatever option is adopted, project sponsors should conduct a **business case** (financial analysis, which in projects should consider risk).

If outside vendors or contractors are being considered, selection of the bidder to build the project (or project components) involves some options. There are a number of bases for selecting a bidder. If the system quality has been thoroughly defined to the extent that every bidder has the knowledge and if each bidder has been screened to ensure their competence, selection on the basis of low bid is usually used. This has obvious advantages, using the competitive system, to lower costs. However, selecting the low bidder has obvious risks if the bidder is not truly qualified. In fact, in some parts of Europe, the winning bidder is the one closest to the average bid, using the logic that they must know what they were asked to do. Regardless, there are other considerations besides low price.

- Cost - need to ensure that it is within the allowable budget
- Feasibility - need to ensure that the bidder can actually do the project
- Experience - look at the bidder's record on similar projects
- Reputation - bidder's record with respect to quality work

Oftentimes, if the bid is too high, the user can negotiate with the bidder. Ethics are involved if an open competitive bidding process was used. Those not selected may not have been treated fairly if the rules are changed after the initial bid. However, in the private sector, this is a legal way to proceed, and the owner and the bidder can work together to negotiate an acceptable agreement for both. Negotiation is appropriate especially when dealing with complex systems when it is attractive to share risks.

In-house systems development begins with the design stage, which involves converting specifications from the definition phase into plans. The proposed system is broken down into subsystems, components, and parts. All elements need to be checked for compatibility, as well as for their ability to meet specifications. Prototyping can be used if there is benefit from seeing what the system will look like.

The system is developed and whatever hardware and software is needed is procured. The system is constructed, and any code and interfaces that are needed are programmed. System testing is conducted concurrently with assembly of the system to catch errors as quickly as possible. Development of training materials is often accomplished concurrently as well.

The production of a system follows analysis and design. The production itself can involve a large group of diverse people, from programmers, people building user interfaces, people designing the database interfaces, people dealing with the users to design reports, and people to set up any required networks for multiple users. The project manager must consider obtaining people with the right skills to be available at the right time, obtaining needed facilities in terms of tools and places to work, realistic time estimates allowing for the appropriate level of uncertainty, and of course capital. Quality testing should be accomplished throughout production. It is a good practice to build systems in modules, and thoroughly test each component before adoption. If at all possible, it would be best to include the user in this testing.

Data Conversion

When a system is developed, data access and input needs to be compatible with the new system. An extreme example of this problem occurs in data mining, where masses of raw data are processed with the intent of obtaining insight into more effective ways of running a business. Data for data mining are almost always stored in data warehouses, capable of storing mammoth quantities of input, such as cash register data. Data conversion is important because for data mining to work, data must be in a usable form, to include having no missing observations, having all data in numeric form, and readable in the proper format. A major element of data warehousing is cleaning data to obtain this state. Executive information systems and enterprise resource planning systems also require data converted to a compatible form.

Testing

Quality control is very important throughout the system development cycle. Each module needs to be checked before a block of work is considered complete. Organizations usually have independent testing groups assigned to review system components to ensure that they are capable of dealing with the expected workload.

Implementation

Once the system is satisfactorily built and tested, it is moved from the builder to the user. This requires that the system be installed and checked out to ensure that it does what was specified. Training the users with technical support available once the system is turned over to the user wraps up the project cycle. The user evaluates system performance and if any flaws are detected, the builder would fix them. Sound contractual agreements spelling out procedures before the project is started are very useful at this stage. Builders often provide maintenance support for systems, usually at some nominal fee. The operation phase includes system improvement.

Summary

Many systems and analysis methods have evolved to support information systems projects. The different methodologies discussed in this chapter all have important roles to play for software projects with specific environmental conditions. Each organization tends to adopt a particular methodology. It is not as important which methodology is adopted as it is that a methodology be adopted. It is also important that software-producing organizations adopt process standards. The SEI/Capability Maturity Model has proven to be dramatically effective at improving process quality and productivity.

Information system project management can involve a wide variety of tasks. Typical information system project types include maintenance work, conversion projects, and new system implementation. Most projects are maintenance related, involving relatively low levels of change. Maintenance of critical activities is often best managed by assigning a permanent team, passing beyond the project stage to a process operation. Conversion work is often required when firms change computer systems, or firms are reorganized. New technology can take a variety of forms, ranging from efficiency-focused transaction processing to software product installation.

Systems development needs to consider cost, time, and performance in addition to specific criteria of importance to a specific project. The activities by system stages were reviewed. Recent research with respect to agile and structured approaches,[1] CMMI usage,[2] and open source project organization[3] are referenced.

Glossary

Agile software development: Methodology emphasizing speed, with a focused team working intensely to bring out a software project to meet an ambitious deadline.

Business case: Financial analysis of a project proposal.

Capability maturity model: Carnegie Mellon rating system for organizational software development maturity.

Charter: Formal document authorizing organizational support for a project.

Data warehousing: Large-scale database technology to organize and store vast quantities of data, enabling data mining analysis.

Decision support systems: Computer systems used to evaluate alternative decision choices.

Enterprise resource planning: Systems designed to provide all organizational MIS needs through integrated, optimized computer software.

Feasibility study: Analysis prior to adoption of a project intended to determine whether the system is doable, within a prescribed budget.

Formal specification: Documentation of project mission and scope.

Implementation phase: Phase of an information systems project where the finished product is put into operation.

Informatics: Business analytics in a contemporary environment, potentially involving access to big data analyzed by machine-learning software.

Internet commerce: Doing business over the Internet.

Make or buy decision: Selecting the alternative among making an information system element with in-house resources, or purchasing the element from a vendor.

Management control: Use of information systems to control an organization.

Outsourcing: Hiring others to do at least part of one's information system.

Process: Activity undertaken to accomplish something the organization needs done.

Prototyping: Testing of a system by developing a small-scale model, so that it can be evaluated.

Rapid prototyping: Use of prototypes with user feedback to quickly identify system weaknesses.

Request for proposal: Formal document outlining project requirements to prospective vendors, asking for their product and associated price.

Scope: Detailed description of the project and/or product, part of the project charter.

Specification phase: Phase of an information systems project where specifications are generated based on requirements analysis.

Statement of work: Formal document specifying standards for a computer software project.

Systems analysis: Function of identifying what an information systems project is intended to do.

Systems design: Result of computer software project design intended to accomplish elements identified in systems analysis.

Systems development approach: Rational way of systematically evaluating information systems projects.

Transaction processing: Use of computer systems to perform repetitive clerical tasks for an organization.

Validation: Process of ensuring that the software performs as designed.

Waterfall model: Systems development cycle consisting of serial activities.

PMBOK Items Relating to Chapter 5:

3.2 Project Management Process Groups

3.9 Role of the Knowledge Areas – ten divisions of concepts, terms, and activities making up a project management field.

   1 Project integration management

   2 Project scope management

   3 Project time management

   4 Project cost management

   5 Project quality management

   6 Project human resource management

   7 Project communications management

   8 Project risk management

9 Project procurement management

10 Project stakeholder management

4.1 Develop Project Charter – the process of developing a document that formally authorizes the existence of a project and provides the project manager with the authority to apply organizational resources to project activities.

5.1 Plan Scope Management - process of creating a scope management plan that documents how the project scope will be defined, validated, and controlled.

5.3 Define Scope – develop detailed description of the project and product.

5.5 Validate Scope – process of formalizing acceptance of the completed project deliverables.

8.1 Plan Quality Management – process of identifying quality requirements and/or standards for the project and its deliverables and documenting how the project will demonstrate compliance with quality requirements.

8.2 Perform Quality Assurance – process of auditing the quality requirements and the results from quality control measurements to ensure that appropriate quality standards and operational definitions are used.

11.1 Plan Risk Management – process of defining how to conduct risk management activities for a project.

11.2 Identify Risks – process of determining which risks may affect the project and documenting their characteristics.

11.3 Perform Qualitative Risk Analysis – process of prioritizing risks for further analysis or action by assessing and combining their probability of occurrence and impact.

11.4 Perform Quantitative Risk Analysis – process of numerically analyzing the effect of identified risks on overall project objectives.

11.5 Plan Risk Responses – process of developing options and actions to enhance opportunities and to reduce threats to project objectives.

References

1   D. Batra, W. Xia, D. VanderMeer, and K. Dutta. 2010. "Balancing Agile and Structured Development Approaches to Successfully Manage Large Distributed Software Projects: A Case Study from the Cruise Line Industry," *Communications of the Association for Information Systems* 27, pp. 379–394.

2   B. Day and C. Lutteroth. 2011. "Climbing the Ladder: Capability Maturity Model Integration Level 3," *Enterprise Information Systems* 5, no. 1, pp. 125–144.

3   A.H. Ghapanchi and A. Aurum. 2012. "The Impact of Project Capabilities on Project Performance: Case of Open Source Software Projects," *International Journal of Project Management* 30, no. 4, pp. 407–417.

PART III

Tools

CHAPTER 6

Estimation

Once a system is developed, more detailed estimating is required. At the strategic level, macroestimates were used to evaluate the project for approval. As the project moves to requirements analysis and determination of feasibility, more accurate estimates are possible as more detailed planning is conducted. During the planning process, detailed tasks (things to do—deliverables) and milestones (completed project module elements, resulting in a completed, functioning system) are identified. This chapter discusses the planning process, as well as factors important in information system project estimation. Several quantitative methods of software project estimation are explained.

Planning Process

Information systems projects have high levels of uncertainty. The size of the project is usually not well understood until systems analysis has been completed. Most of the unexpected delay in these projects occurs during the latter stages of testing, late in the project. Systems builders tend to report projects as on time and budget targets until the last stages of testing. But at this point, most projects are found to require additional work, often substantial in scope.

Information systems projects have several unique factors that lead to high variability in project durations, including variances in the productivity across people for specific work, and in the technology used. Resources available are often not known at the beginning of a project. Many specific resources may be planned for use on a project during the planning stages, but months later other events may arise that make it impossible to use the best people on a project.

The planning process consists of a number of steps, including:

- determining requirements
- identifying specific work to be done
- planning project organization
- scheduling
- budgeting resources
- establishing control mechanisms.

Set Objectives and Requirements

The first step is to determine requirements. Project objectives are set in the early stages of project proposals. Once these objectives are identified, the measures of accomplishment needed to identify successful completion of the project have to be established. These are the standards for each element of the project. In building a bridge, this would be the carrying capacity of the structure. In terms of information systems projects, this would be a statement of what the final project is ultimately supposed to do.

A **statement of work**, which we introduced in Chapter 5, can be viewed as a contract between the information systems development team and project end users (see Figure 6.1). The statement of work can contain product descriptions, discussion of project constraints, schedule requirements, budget limits, and an explanation of the roles and responsibilities of project participants.

Constraints under which the system must be developed should be identified early in the project. These include time parameters, such as deadlines. The project may have to be accomplished within existing skill levels. Levels of project complexity can be specified. Budgets are an important resource limitation. Technology might be imposed, such as using CASE tools. Interoperability opportunities, such as the availability of proprietary or open systems, may be specified.

Specify Work Activities

A **work breakdown structure** is a top-down hierarchical chart of tasks and subtasks required to complete the project (see Figure 6.2). The work

Statement of Work for: **Installation of Decision Support System for Purchasing Manager**

This system is to provide the Purchasing Manager support in considering vendors for any external material purchased by Acme Distilleries.

The system is to consist of:

a. the necessary hardware for a personal computer station, monitor and speakers, capable of linking to the management local area network;

> This system is to have the following technical specifications:
>> 1.0-GHz processor
>> 2-GB onboard memory, configurable to 4 GB
>> 256-GB flash storage
>> 13-in. LED-backlit glossy widescreen display
>> USB bus.

b. standard operating software;

c. specialty software to include a database, as well as room for vendor price quotations;

d. a backup drive.

The system is to be installed no later than October 4, 2015.

The base system cost is not to exceed $10,000.

Any proposed changes will be priced by the system builder and presented to the user, who will decide if the proposed changes should be adopted. The user will fund these changes at the stated price.

Figure 6.1 Statement of work

breakdown structure can be focused on a product, a function, or anything describing what needs to be accomplished. The work breakdown structure is hierarchical, in that different levels of detail can be described. The overall project consists of a set of major activities, or project sub-elements. The schedule consists of a set of tasks, usually denoting work done by a specific worker or work group. This is usually the lowest level of project activity that is used for planning. In Figure 5.2, task "System Design" is a major task with four sub-elements at two levels. Sub-activity "Design Software System to Support Work Process" consists of three unique sub-activities. Task "Installation" consists of only one level of five activities. For large projects, quite a few levels in the work breakdown structure hierarchy may be required.

A **detailed task list** is a listing of unique work packages, briefly describing work to be done. The detailed task list also includes the assignment of responsibilities by job title, and predecessor relationships. Predecessor relationships identify the conditions required for tasks to begin. Resources required, deliverables, and estimated durations are also provided. Figure 6.3 demonstrates a detailed task list for an example project. This information makes it possible to schedule and plan the project.

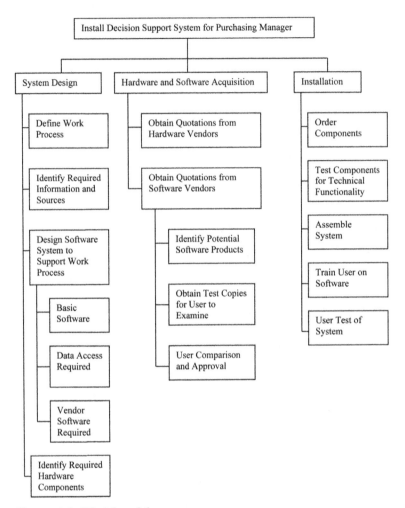

Figure 6.2 Work breakdown structure

The work packages for tasks can include a summary of work to be done, predecessors (activities that must be completed before this task can be started), who is responsible, specifications for output, resources required, and deliverables. In Figure 5.3, predecessors and durations are provided for those tasks that are not subdivided. Specifications or required output could be provided as needed.

This detailed task list is the basis for estimating, scheduling, and allocating resources. The time required to accomplish each task, as well as the resources required by task, are included. Identifying these numbers

Project: Installation of Decision Support System for Purchasing Manager

Tasks	Subtasks	Responsible Parties	Predecessors
A	System Design		
A1	Define work process	system engineer, user	none
A2	Identify required information and sources	system engineer, user	A1
A3	Design software system to support work process		
A31	Basic software	assistant	A2
A32	Data access required	assistant, user	A2
A33	Vendor software required	assistant, user	A2
A4	Identify required hardware components	system engineer, user	A31, A32, A33
A0	System Design Milestone		A4
B	Hardware and Software Acquisition		
B1	Obtain quotations from hardware vendors	hardware acquisition	A0
B2	Obtain quotations from software vendors		
B21	Identify potential software products	software acquisition	A0
B22	Obtain test copies for user to examine	software acquisition	B21
B23	User comparison and approval	system engineer, user	B22
B0	Hardware and Software Acquisition Milestone		B1, B23
C	Installation		
C1	Order components	software acquisition	B0
C2	Test components for technical functionality	assistant	C1
C3	Assemble system	assistant	C2
C4	Train user on software	trainer, user	C3
C5	User test of system	system engineer, user	C4
C0	Installation Milestone		C5

Task	Resources Required	Deliverable	Estimated Duration
A1	system engineer, user	document describing work process	2 days
A2	system engineer, user	list of required information sources	1 day
A31	system engineer	document describing system	3 days
A32	system engineer, user	list of data access required	1 day
A33	system engineer, user	list of software required	1 day
A4	system engineer, user	document formally identifying components	2 days
B1	hardware acquisition	list of specifications with prices	2 days
B21	software acquisition	list of software available with prices	4 days
B22	software acquisition	examination copies	10 days
B23	system engineer, user	user approval	5 days
C1	software acquisition	purchase orders	3 days
C2	system engineer	letters of certification	2 days
C3	system engineer	functioning system	1 day
C4	trainer, user	trainer certification	2 days
C5	system engineer, user	user signed approval	3 days

Figure 6.3 Detailed task list

is the task of **estimation** at this stage. Accurate estimation is a very difficult task. The best way to increase accuracy is to rely on experience supplemented by careful study and record keeping. It is wise to build a database of norms based on past experiences for reference in estimating future projects. Any project environment involves difficulty in estimating, because by their nature, projects involve dealing with new activities. This is true especially in the field of information systems, because of the phenomenal rate of change in technology.

There is a natural human tendency to "pad" estimates of the time required to do things. If your professor asks you how long it will take you to write a ten page paper, would you respond with the fastest time you have ever written such a paper? You would not even respond with the average time you have taken to write such a paper. You would most likely respond with an estimate that you felt was safe. If you ask a programmer how long it will take to write a specific piece of code, you will probably receive an estimate that the programmer expects to beat 80 or 90 percent of the time. The programmer's supervisor will in turn probably add an inflationary factor to allow for contingencies, like having to use a slower programmer. This continues up the chain of command until the final estimate is made. Everyone, even management, realizes that the estimate is padded. Management then adjusts for this padding by CUTTING the estimate drastically. What results is a wild guess that may or may not have much relationship to reality.

A due date can become a self-fulfilling prophecy. If an activity actually takes less time than the due date, work is usually slowed until the due date becomes accurate. Due dates thus can have a negative impact on project performance.

Those doing the work need to be convinced that accurate estimates are in their best interest (the ability of the firm to accurately estimate what is required to do work, so that they can submit competitive yet realistic prices for project work). The focus should rather be on the chain of critical activities and those activities that might become critical. (The critical chain consists of those activities which cannot be delayed without delaying the project completion time.) This is accomplished by close management attention to make sure adequate resources are provided to critical activities, and frequent reporting of the need to finish this critical work to those who are doing it.

It is very easy for estimators to be overly optimistic. At the beginning of a project, it is natural to assume that everything will work as planned. But because of the need to accomplish a wide variety of tasks, and their interrelationships, projects rarely proceed as scheduled. Rarely will things go faster than planned. This is because of the need to obtain approval of end users, and the need for delivery of materials and other components.

Plan Project Organization

Organizing refers to identifying the roles in the project organization. A **responsibility matrix** is a way to allocate tasks to individuals by responsibility (see Figure 6.4). Such a matrix can be invaluable in complex projects, enabling management to quickly identify who is responsible for each activity. This matrix can also be used when forming the project team, enabling identification of what needs to be done for comparison with the capabilities of candidates.

An **organization chart** shows the reporting relationships of all involved in the project. Figure 6.5 shows the organization for the project we have been demonstrating. The organization chart outlines the communication network and coordination patterns required within the project as well. Within matrix organizational forms, this organization chart should show both primary and secondary reporting relationships. This can include not only those temporarily assigned from functional elements to the project, but also external relationships, such as the project owner, and vendors.

RACI charts are often used to clearly define roles and responsibilities. RACI stands for Responsible, Accountable, Consult, and Inform. Responsible individuals own the project element. For a given activity, no more than one individual should be assigned responsibility. Accountable people are given the task of completing the activity, in support of the responsible individual. Consulting personnel are those with expertise needed to accomplish the project, available to support the responsible and accountable people. Inform people are those who need to know project status. Figure 6.6 displays a RACI chart for the project outlined in Figure 6.4:

Project: Installation of Decision Support System for Purchasing Manager

Tasks	Subtasks	SE	HA	SA	TR	user
A System Design						
A1	Define work process	x				x
A2	Identify required information and sources	x				x
A3	Design software system to support work process					
A31	Basic software	x				
A32	Data access required	x				x
A33	Vendor software required	x				x
A4	Identify required hardware components	x				x
A0	System Design Milestone					
B Hardware and Software Acquisition						
B1	Obtain quotations from hardware vendors		x			
B2	Obtain quotations from software vendors			x		
B21	Identify potential software products			x		
B22	Obtain test copies for user to examine			x		
B23	User comparison and approval	x				x
B0	Hardware and Software Acquisition Milestone					
C Installation						
C1	Order components			x		
C2	Test components for technical functionality	x				
C3	Assemble system	x				
C4	Train users on software				x	x
C5	User test of system	x				x
C0	Installation Milestone					

KEY: SE   software engineer
HA   hardware acquisition
SA   software acquisition
TR   trainer

Figure 6.4 Responsibility matrix

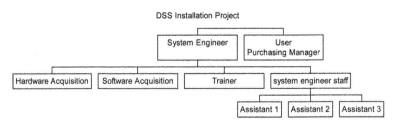

Figure 6.5 Organization chart

Task	Description	SE	HA	SA	TR	User
A1	Define work process	A				R
A2	Identify required information and sources	R				C
A31	Basic software	R		C		
A32	Data access required	R		C		C
A33	Vendor software required	C	I	R	I	I
A4	Identify required hardware components	C	R			
B1	Obtain quotations from hardware vendors		R			
B21	Identify potential software products			R		
B22	Obtain test copies for user to examine			R		
B23	User comparison and approval	C		C	I	R
C1	Order components	I	I	R	I	
C2	Test components for technical functionality	R	C	C		
C3	Assemble system	R	C	C		
C4	Train users on software				R	C
C5	User test of system	C	I	I	I	R

Figure 6.6 RACI chart

Develop the Schedule

Schedules consist of the sequence of tasks from the work breakdown structure, along with their start and completion dates, and relationships to other tasks (see Figure 6.7). Schedules include not only time estimates but also resource requirements. Microsoft Project allows display of resources to the right of the bar representing the planned activity schedule. Schedules give everyone an understandable plan and impose structure on the project, and should therefore be widely distributed among members of the project team.

Schedules are the basis for resource allocation and estimated cost for monitoring and control purposes. The focus is on identifying when activities (tasks) are completed, so that work can proceed on following activities.

Control Points

Control points include milestones, check point reviews, status review meetings, and staff meetings. When planning the project, control

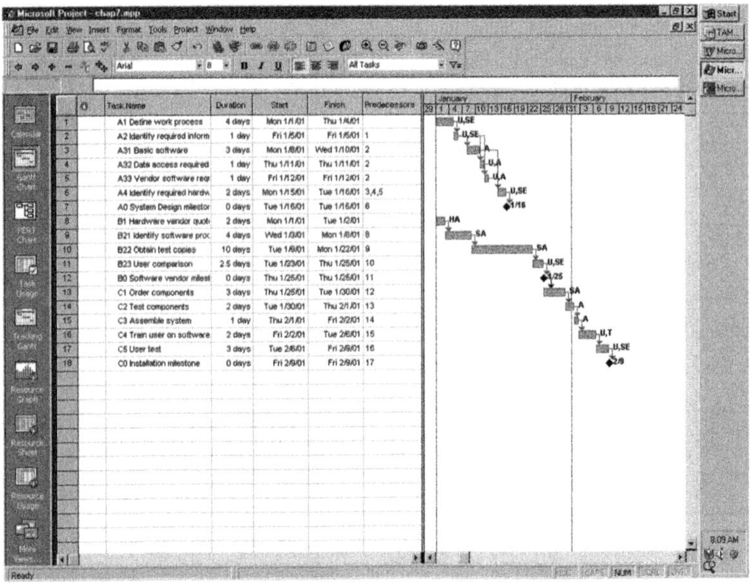

Figure 6.7 Project schedule

mechanisms should also be included. Because of the existence of inter-related activities, **milestone** events are often used at the end of particular phases, or groupings of activities resulting in the completion of project subcomponents. Meetings are an important control device, providing a way to keep each element of the organization informed of what is going on. In Figure 6.7, activities 7 (System Design milestone), 12 (Software vendor milestone), and 18 (Installation milestone) are milestone activities.

There are three types of meetings that are often useful in information systems projects. **Checkpoint reviews** are held at the conclusion of each phase to determine whether or not to proceed with the rest of the project. In information system projects, this is the appropriate time to test the performance of the completed component. If its performance is less than planned, it may be necessary to change the rest of the project, and possibly even cancel it. **Status review meetings** are used to gather cost, quality, and schedule information. These give project management the measures needed to control the project. Finally, **staff meetings** are regularly held to maintain communication.

The primary purpose of budgets is to give management control over expenditures. A key activity is tracking actual expenditures relative to the budget. Variance reports are often used to focus on those project elements that are in the greatest amount of difficulty. When such problems are encountered, plans need to be developed to adjust to the new circumstances.

Resource usage can be measured by time period. Figure 6.8 demonstrates the schedule for the user representative before leveling, as displayed by Microsoft Project. The week beginning January 7 has a problem, with the user representative assigned to two activities at once (A32 and A33). In the plan shown in Figure 6.7, the project completion was delayed one day to allow the user representative to participate in both activities. Most if not all project management software provides similar tools to flag when available resources are overscheduled.

The planning process is key to accurate cost estimation, which in turn is required for sound managerial decision making about project adoption. This is true especially for consulting organizations, which price bids to potential customers. In a competitive environment, bidding too high results in no work. Bidding too low is even worse, because it leads to undertaking projects at a loss, and ultimately can lead to bankruptcy. To accurately know what the cost of delivering a project

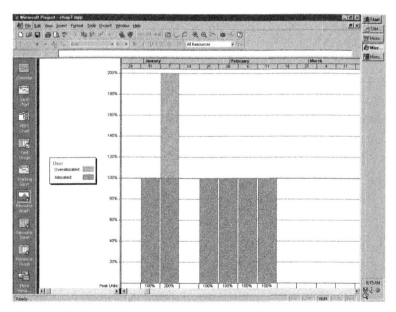

Figure 6.8 Microsoft project resource usage chart

will be, you need to know the resources required. In a complex project, the duration that these resources are needed for is very difficult to estimate without a good database of the time similar activities took in the past, and analysis and understanding of special conditions that could affect these durations.

Software Estimation Methods

Software estimation is a very difficult task. The most commonly used approaches are based on source lines of code (SLOC, or LOC). The number of lines of code seems to be of less and less importance as productivity tools are developed, and more productive languages are used. One attempt to base estimation on more relevant project features is function point (FP) analysis, which focuses on the functions the proposed system needs to accomplish. However, most research has not found any improvement in estimation through use of FP analysis in practice. SLOC is still widely used, and is the basis of the constructive cost model (COCOMO) system covered below. While these systems have noted flaws, estimating methods significantly better have not been widely reported.

The software production cycle can be described in many ways. A simple view consists of the following major elements: design and development, production, testing, installation, and maintenance.

The size of the system has been found to be an important variable in the cost and time required to develop software. Size can be measured on a number of dimensions. The most commonly used are the amount of information processed, technical requirements, and performance drivers (cost, time, and quality).

The amount of time required to develop a set of code is a function of its size. The following demonstration of the source lines of code (SLOC or LOC) and FP methods demonstrates this point.

Lines of Code

Both LOC and FP methods begin with the scientifically sound approach of gathering historical records of experiences of past projects. These historical data are the basis for identifying the relationship between key measures of importance (such as the person-months of effort and dollars

Lines of Code Operation						
Averages of past projects: Effort	$(000)	pp. Doc.	Errors	defects	people
LOC	20,543 33 mos.	361	1194	201	52	4
average per KLOC	1.606	15.673	58.122	9.784	2.531	0.195
SLOC: estimate lines of code, multiply						

Figure 6.9 Lines of code calculation

expended) and other factors of importance (such as the pages of documentation generated, errors encountered, system defects, and people assigned). An implementation of the LOC approach (Figure 6.9) uses the following key measures per line of code.

When a new project is encountered, an estimate is made of the lines of code that the project will require. For instance, if a new project is estimated to involve 10,000 lines of code, estimates of these measures would be as given in Table 6.1:

This approach is admittedly rough, but provides a very easy way to implement estimation method. While gathering the data is time consuming, once it is obtained, it is very quick. It will be more accurate the more appropriate the data are, of course. Ideally, firms could build their database in categories by type of work, as averaging radically different projects together will lead to obvious inaccuracies. Another limitation is that it takes time to generate a database of historical project results. As with any statistical approach, the more data, the greater the confidence. However, the older the data, the less likely they are appropriate to current operations. Additionally, the model as demonstrated is totally linear, while project size may have different impacts at different size levels. More refined methods have been developed.

Table 6.1 Application of LOC

Effort	1.606 × 10 thousand LOC	=	16 person-months
Budget	15.673 × "	=	$157,000
Documentation	58.122 × "	=	581 pages
Errors	9.784 × "	=	98
Defects	2.531 × "	=	25
People	0.195 × "	=	2 people

Function Point Analysis

Albrecht's Function Point Analysis Method supplements these project size bases of estimation. The aims of this approach are a consistent measure meaningful to the end user with rules that are easy to apply. The method can be used to estimate cost and time based upon requirement specifications, and is independent of the technology used.

The FP method works in a very similar way to lines of code, except that the basis for estimation is FP (reflecting in essence work to do). The original FP method involved counts of the number of activities in five categories (user inputs, user outputs, user inquiries, files accessed, and external interfaces). The number of functions is counted by complexity level for each factor, and multiplied as in Figure 6.10:

The count-total is the sum of the product column. To demonstrate on a hypothetical software proposal, see Figure 6.11:

The next step is to calculate F_i, which is calculated by adding the ratings over the following 14 factors on a 0–5 scale, with 0 representing no impact, 1 incidental, 2 moderate, 3 average, 4 significant, and 5 essential impact. The calculation, with a hypothetical set of impacts, is shown in Figure 6.12:

FPs are then calculated by the formula:

$$FP = \text{count-total} \times [0.65 + 0.01 \times \Sigma F_i]$$

In the hypothetical example, estimation of effort would be:

$$FP = 494 \times [0.65 + 0.01 \times 32] = 479.18$$

Count-Total Calculations				
		Complexity Weighting		
Measurement Parameter	Low	Average	High	product
Number of user inputs	_____ × 3 +	_____ × 4 +	_____ × 6	= _____
Number of user outputs	_____ × 4 +	_____ × 5 +	_____ × 7	= _____
Number of user inquiries	_____ × 3 +	_____ × 4 +	_____ × 6	= _____
Number of files	_____ × 7 +	_____ × 10 +	_____ × 15	= _____
Number of external interfaces	_____ × 5 +	_____ × 7 +	_____ × 10	= _____

Figure 6.10 Function point count calculations

Demonstration of Count-Total Calculation

Software: A bank accounts record system involving:

36 user inputs	classified as simple in complexity
5 user outputs	classified as average in complexity
20 possible user inquiries	classified as simple in complexity
40 files accessed	classified as simple in complexity
3 external interfaces	classified as average in complexity

Measurement Parameter	count	simple	average	complex	product
Number of user inputs	36	× 3			108
Number of user outputs	5		× 5		25
Number of user inquiries	20	× 3			60
Number of files	40	× 7			280
Number of external interfaces	3		× 7		21
				Total	494

Figure 6.11 Count-total calculation

Function Calculation Demonstration

	1–5 scale
F1 Does the system require reliable backup and recovery?	Significant (4)
F2 Are data communications required?	Moderate (2)
F3 Are there distributed processing functions?	Significant (4)
F4 Is performance critical?	Average (3)
F5 Will the system run in an existing, heavily utilized operational environment?	Essential (5)
F6 Does the system require online data entry?	Essential (5)
F7 Does the online data entry require the input transactionon multiple screens or operations?	Incidental (1)
F8 Are the master files updated online?	No influence (0)
F9 Are the inputs, outputs, files, or inquiries complex?	Incidental (1)
F10 Is the internal processing complex?	Incidental (1)
F11 Is the code designed to be reusable?	Average (3)
F12 Are conversion and installation included in the design?	Average (3)
F13 Is the system designed for multiple installations in different organizations?	No influence (0)
F14 Is the application designed to facilitate change and ease of use by the user?	No influence (0)
Total F	32

Figure 6.12 Function calculation

Function Point Estimation						
Averages of past projects:	Effort	$(000)	pp. Doc.	Errors	defects	people
FP 623	33 mos.	361	1194	201	52	4
average per FP	0.05297	0.57945	1.91653	0.32263	0.08347	0.00642
FUNCTION POINTS: calculate FP, multiply averages by 479.18						
	Effort	$(000)	pp. Doc	Errors	defects	people
479.18 ×	0.05297	0.57945	1.91653	0.32263	0.08347	0.00642
yields estimates	25.4	278	918	155	40	3

Figure 6.13 Function point estimate

Then the estimation of required resources (Figure 6.13) would be similar to that for LOC:

While lines of code have proven useful, and while the FP method is also useful and widely used, estimation of software project effort continues to be a difficult task. Many other approaches continue to be generated. In part, new developments are needed because the software project environment is changing, with far less reliance on actual coding (the most predictable part of a software project).

The next model applies logarithmic regression on past data to more accurately reflect the time required to accomplish code development. COCOMO reflects the impact of learning, in that as the project progresses, programmers and developers are expected to gain in the rate of productivity.

Constructive Cost Model

Constructive cost models (COCOMO) for estimating the effort required for developing software have been promulgated. The basic COCOMO model computes software development effort based on program size. An intermediate model also considers a set of cost drivers reflecting specific product, hardware, personnel, and project characteristics. The advanced model breaks out cost driver impact on each step of the software engineering process.

For relatively small, simple software projects built by small teams with good experience, COCOMO formulas for person-months of effort and development time in chronological months are:

$$\text{Person-months} = 2.4 \times \text{KLOC}^{1.05} = \text{E for effort}$$
$$\text{Duration (months)} = 2.5 \times \text{E}^{0.38}$$

Thus, for a job of this type involving 50,000 lines of code,

$$\text{Person-months} = 2.4 \times 50^{1.05} = 145.925 \text{ months}$$
$$\text{Duration} = 2.5 \times 145.925^{0.38} = 16.6 \text{ months}$$

For software projects of intermediate size and complexity, built by teams with mixed experience and facing more rigid than average requirements, the formulas are:

$$\text{Person-months} = 3.0 \times \text{KLOC}^{1.12}$$
$$\text{Duration (months)} = 2.5 \times \text{E}^{0.35}$$

Therefore, a job of this type involving 50,000 lines of code would have the following estimates:

$$\text{Person-months} = 3.0 \times 50^{1.12} = 239.865 \text{ months}$$
$$\text{Duration} = 2.5 \times 239.865^{0.35} = 17.0 \text{ months}$$

Finally, for a software project built under rigid conditions, the formulas are:

$$\text{Person-months} = 3.6 \times \text{KLOC}^{1.2}$$
$$\text{Duration (months)} = 2.5 \times \text{E}^{0.32}$$

A job involving 50,000 lines of code under these conditions would be estimated:

$$\text{Person-months} = 3.6 \times 50^{1.2} = 393.610 \text{ months}$$
$$\text{Duration} = 2.5 \times 393.610^{0.32} = 16.9 \text{ months}$$

There are variations in COCOMO. Companies could generate their own using regression on their productivity data. There are many causes of productivity loss. For one thing, the amount of time applied by humans to actual coding is only about 20 hours per week, due to machine downtime, emergency diversion, meetings, paperwork, sick time, and many other factors. A great deal of this waste is recovered by using automated tools, except for machine downtime.

Interactions are activities involving coordination with others. The more interactions, the less productivity. High-level languages increase productivity by almost eliminating the programming component, but the more unpredictable activities still have to be accomplished by the project team.

Planning for Change

As we stated at the outset of the prior section, software estimation methods have been found wanting. LOC would seem to be irrelevant to contemporary system development environments, but FP analysis does not appear to be much better. As we also said at the beginning of the prior section, these methods appear to be about as good as anything at estimating software projects. Therefore, systems developers can expect high levels of change in project development duration.

Given the pace of technological business change, systems should be developed with anticipation of change. The prototyping approach, where a working version of the system is built before final design, is appropriate for some projects, where the idea is to design the product's final details AFTER seeing a mock-up in action. Development principles that make sense in this environment include modularization, sub-routing, documentation of interfaces, and high-level languages.

There are a number of implementations of risk analysis in software development. Buffer approaches will be discussed in Chapter 7. Another approach is to identify threats to project completion with respect to time, budget, and quality, and development of contingency plans to be implemented should these threats materialize. One obvious contingency plan is to cancel the project should it encounter too many unexpected delays and budget overruns. Other contingency alternatives are to pull internal experts off other projects to get this project back on track. Outsourcing can also be used, retaining external experts from the consulting field.

Scheduling

It is a rule of thumb that coding is 90 percent finished for about half of the time it was in process. Debugging was estimated to be 99 percent complete most of the time it was underway. You probably have written a computer code, and should understand this very well. Humans are optimistic. The time required for computer tasks are very difficult to estimate accurately.

In studies of government projects, where estimates were carefully updated every two weeks, there was very little change in estimated duration until the activity actually started. While the activity was underway, those activities that actually took less time than the estimate dropped, to reflect the new knowledge. On the other hand, when things were clearly going to take longer than estimated, the estimates were rarely changed until deep into the activity.

Milestones are concrete events denoting the completion of a project phase. When a phase of project activity (a set of related tasks, such as completion of all system design tasks in Figure 6.3) is finished, to include successful component testing, a milestone is completed. Milestones are scheduled as activities with zero duration, reflecting completion of a block of work.

Critical path models, to be elaborated on in Chapter 7, are network descriptions of project activities that identify activity start times and completion times. Brooks found preparation of critical path models to be their most valuable aspect. Dependencies are clearly identified, and there is value in estimating activity durations. Critical path models were meant to aid project control by allowing comparison of actual performance with planned performance. However, as a control device, model elements such as task completion status are often not updated until too late, at which time the system change is dramatic. When delay is first noticed, the tendency is not to report it. Project management systems provide status information giving the latest reported picture of what is going on. The key to successful management is determining when something needs to be done to correct what is going on.

Summary

Estimation of activity duration and cost is key to sound scheduling and budgeting. It is a very difficult task, because project activities are so variable in these terms.

A great deal of effort has been given to accurately estimate software development projects. Specific measures of project size include source lines of code (SLOC or LOC), the most commonly used measurement. This method is based on a concrete measure, which is attractive. But it is deficient in that it is often difficult to specify the specific lines in question. Different languages can require very different approaches for different tasks. In former times, when FORTRAN was the standard language for numerical computation and when COBOL was the standard for data processing, estimates of lines of code were quite consistent. Now, however, with the many productivity tools available and a much greater variety of languages used, lines of code are not as useful as measures. FPs focus more on what software is intended to do. COCOMO reflects learning aspects of software productivity. While all of these methods provide some insight into the time an information systems project might take, each has limitations. Two recent research pieces on software project estimation are referenced.[1]

A sound estimating procedure would identify the work to be done (the work breakdown structure), estimated the time required by resource, and estimate the money required to pay the required people or hire the required consultants or equipment. To that, time-independent items such as materials or external purchases can be added. Overhead can then be allocated following company policies.

Uncertainty is a major factor with respect to the time project activities will take. Cost is often correlated with time. Most delays are incurred in the testing phase, late in the project. It is even rarer for a project to take less time than originally estimated. This in great part is due to the human factor of rechecking work if it is completed early, or sometimes stalling. Projects have on occasion been completed ahead of schedule, but not very often.

Glossary

Checkpoint reviews: Meetings held at the conclusion of each project phase to determine whether the rest of the project should be completed, or if modifications to the project are required.

Constructive cost model (COCOMO): Software project estimation method based on a nonlinear regression against lines of code.

Detailed task list: listing of work packages briefly describing work to be done.

Function point analysis method: Software project estimation method based on the functions the software is designed to accomplish.

Lines of cod: Software project estimation method based on extrapolation from the estimated lines of code required.

Milestone: Distinct event signifying completion of a block of tasks.

Organization chart: Hierarchical sketch of reporting relationships among the people in an organization.

Planning process: Steps of information systems project management to systematically establish work activities, their schedules, budgets, and control mechanisms.

RACI chart: Display of responsibility and accountability by individual, as well as identifying those who should be consulted or informed for each project activity or sub-activity.

Responsibility matrix: Chart identifying individuals responsible for project tasks.

SLOC: Simple lines of code—see Lines of Code.

Statement of work: Document describing what a system is to do in terms of functionality.

Status review meetings: Meetings to update project participants about project status, as well as to gather cost, quality, and time information.

Work breakdown structure: Hierarchical chart of tasks required to accomplish a project.

PMBOK Items Relating to Chapter 6:

3.1 Common project management processes are guides for applying appropriate project management knowledge and skills during the project.

3.3 Initiating Process Group—processes performed to define a new project or a new phase of an existing project by obtaining authorization to start.

3.4 Planning Process Group—those processes performed to establish the total scope of the effort, define and refine the objectives, and develop the course of action required to attain those objectives.

3.8 Project Information—data and information collected, analyzed, transformed, and distributed to project team members and other stakeholders.

4.2 Develop Project Management Plan—the process of defining, preparing, and coordinating all subsidiary plans and integrating them into a comprehensive project management plan.

5.2 Collect Requirements—process of determining, documenting, and managing the stakeholder needs and requirements to meet project objectives.

5.3 Define Scope—process of documenting project features and constraints.

5.4 Create WBS—process of subdividing project deliverables and project work into smaller, more manageable components.

6.4 Estimate Activity Resources—process of estimating the type and quantities of material, human resources, equipment, or supplies required to perform each activity.

6.5 Estimate Activity Durations—process of estimating the number of work periods needed to complete individual activities with estimated resources.

7.2 Estimate Costs—process of developing an approximation of the monetary resources needed to complete project activities.

7.3 Determine Budget—process of aggregating the estimated costs of individual activities or work packages to establish an authorized cost baseline.

Reference

1   N. Nunes, L. Constantine, and R. Kazman. 2011. "iUCP: Estimating Interactive-Software Project Size with Enhanced Use-Case Points," *IEEE Software* 28, no. 4, pp. 64–73; C. Symons. 2012. "Exploring Software Project Effort versus Duration Trade-offs," *IEEE Software* 29, no. 4, pp. 67–74.

CHAPTER 7

Quantitative Project Scheduling Methods

The Critical Path Method

The critical path method provides a way to easily identify the fastest a project can be completed, given that the estimated durations of activities are accurate. Even though estimated durations are usually at variance with actual outcomes, the critical path method provides a useful analysis of which activities are time bottlenecks. The input to the critical path method is a list of each activity, its expected duration, and those activities that immediately precede this activity. "Immediately precede" in this case means that predecessor activities must be completed before the subject activity can begin, and there are no other activities between the predecessor and the activity in question.

The **critical path method** provides a basis for identifying the criticality of specific activities, which can help determine which among competing activities can be delayed to stay within resource levels. A **critical activity** is an activity that must be completed on schedule or else project completion time will be delayed. Therefore, critical activities are said to have no **slack**, or spare time to complete. A **critical path** is the chain of critical activities from the beginning of the project to project completion. If a project has no overall slack between the time it is to be completed and the minimum time to complete based on duration estimates, there will be at least one critical path for the project. However, there may be multiple critical paths, or more than one sequence of activities related by predecessor/follower relationships that have zero slack. To demonstrate, consider the following very simple project, consisting of five activities as shown in Table 7.1.

Table 7.1 Demonstration activity list

Activity	Duration (Weeks)	Predecessors
A Estimate cost to complete project	12	None
B Bid job and complete contract	1	A
C Build system	40	B
D Develop training	20	B
E Implement system	5	C, D

Figure 7.1 displays a Gantt chart of this project.

Another graphical output of the critical path method is a **Gantt chart**, which displays the early start schedule versus time (Figure 7.1). In this case, it is clear that there is only one critical path, consisting of the chain of activities A–B–C–E. Activity D has slack.

This is all of the information required to develop a critical path model. The critical path algorithm is quite straightforward.

Early Start Schedule

An early start schedule (first pass) is developed (Table 7.2). For every activity which has no unscheduled predecessors, schedule the activity to start as soon as possible (either the project start time, or the maximum early finish of all predecessors). The critical path schedules are optimal with respect to time. This process continues until all activities are scheduled. The early finish is the sum of the early start time plus the duration.

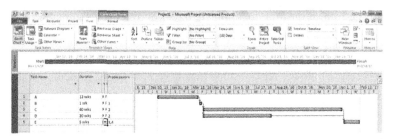

Figure 7.1 Gantt chart from Microsoft Project

Table 7.2 Early start schedule

Activity	Early Start	Early Finish	
A Estimate cost to complete project	0	12	Releases B
B Bid job and complete contract	12	12 + 1 = 13	Releases C and D
C Build system	13	13 + 40 = 53	
D Develop training	13	13 + 20 = 33	With C, releases E
E Implement system	MAX(53,33)	53 + 5 = 58	

The project **early completion time** is the maximum early finish. In this case the project early completion time is 58 weeks.

Networks

Quite often a **network** is displayed, which graphically displays the relationship between activities (Figure 7.2). Networks are not really needed for development of early start schedules, but are very useful in sorting out the relationships for late start schedules. They also provide a valuable visual aid for managers to identify relationships among activities.

Late Start Schedule

The next phase of the critical path analysis is the **late start schedule** (second pass). The late start schedule is the latest an activity can be scheduled without delaying project completion time. The final ending

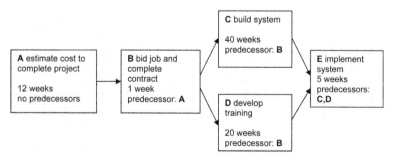

Figure 7.2 Network

Table 7.3 Late start schedule

Activity	Late Finish	Late Start	
A Estimate cost to complete project	58	58 − 5 = 53	Releases C and D
B Bid job and complete contract	53	53 − 20 = 33	
C Build system	53	53 − 40 = 13	With D, releases B
D Develop training	MIN (13, 33)	13 − 1 = 12	Releases A
E Implement system	12	12 − 12 = 0	

time for the project can be some contract deadline, which may be different from the early finish schedule, or the early finish project completion time can be used. If the deadline is earlier than the project early finish time, the project is infeasible (cannot be completed on time with given durations). If the deadline is later than the project early finish time, all activities in the project will have slack, or spare time. If the deadline coincides with the project early finish time, there will be at least one **critical path**, connecting activities in a chain with zero slack.

The late start schedule (Table 7.3) is calculated in reverse. Begin with the end time (deadline or early finish time). All activities that do not appear on the list of predecessors for unscheduled activities can be scheduled. The late finish time will be either the project end time, or the minimum of the late start times for all following activities.

Slack

Slack (**float**) is the difference between the late start and early start schedules (it doesn't matter which you use, because in both cases the difference between them is the duration). Those activities with zero slack are critical. If they are delayed, the project completion time will be delayed. There can be more than one critical path for a project, and the project network presented in Figure 7.2 can be useful in assuring identification of each critical path. Calculations are given in Table 7.4:

Table 7.4 Slack calculations

Activity	Early Start	Early Finish	Late Start	Late Finish	Slack	
A Estimate cost to complete project	0	12	0	12	0	Critical
B Bid job and complete contract	12	13	12	13	0	Critical
C Build system	13	53	13	53	0	Critical
D Develop training	13	33	33	53	20	
E Implement system	53	58	53	58	0	Critical

Table 7.5 Second example project

Activity	Duration	Predecessors
A Rough design of advertising plan	1 week	None
B Convince project manager	3 weeks	A
C Develop marketing plan	3 weeks	B
D Identify media alternatives	2 weeks	B
E Print materials	1 week	C
F Brief sales force	2 weeks	B
G Select media	1 week	D

Slack in the case above exists for only one activity, D. More complex projects will include slack for multiple activities, such as the following project (Table 7.5).

This project has the following slacks (Table 7.6):

Table 7.6 Slacks for second project

Activity	Early Start	Early Finish	Late Start	Late Finish	Slack	
A Rough design of advertising plan	0	1	0	1	0	Critical
B Convince product manager	1	4	1	4	0	Critical
C Develop marketing plan	4	7	4	7	0	Critical
D Identify media alternatives	4	6	5	7	1	
E Print materials	7	8	7	8	0	Critical
F Brief sales force	4	6	6	8	2	
G Select media	6	7	7	8	1	

		W	E	E	K	S			
Activity	Duration	1	2	3	4	5	6	7	8
A rough design of advertising plan	1 week	■							
B convince product manager	3 weeks		■	■	■				
C develop marketing plan	3 weeks					■	■	■	
D identify media alternatives	2 weeks					■	■	s	
E print materials	1 week								■
F brief sales force	2 weeks					■	■	s	s
G select media	1 week							■	s
	Scheduled	■							
	Slack	s							
	Critical	■							

Figure 7.3 Gantt chart

A Gantt chart for this project is shown in Figure 7.3.

In this case, activities D, G, and F all have one unit of slack. Looking at the Gantt chart for this project, it is clear that activity F is independent of D and G, so that if a week is lost in briefing the sales force, it interferes with nothing else. This case is **independent slack** (free float). On the other hand, if identifying media alternatives should take an extra week, the slack of 1 week is shared with that of activity G, which would become critical if the slack on activity D were used up. This case is **shared slack.**

Project management software includes the ability to have a number of precedence relationships. The default is generally predecessor finish = follower start. Other options include predecessor start = follower start, or predecessor start = follower start plus some lag time.

The critical path method provides a useful means of identifying the earliest a project can be completed, as well as identifying those activities that are critical. Critical activities need to be managed more closely than slack activities. This is because if any delay is experienced on a critical activity, the project completion time will be delayed. On the other hand, if things are delayed for activity D in our first example, it doesn't really matter until 20 spare days are wasted. However, one should be careful, because once all of an activity's slack is exhausted, it also becomes critical.

There is a bias in projects, in that activity delays accumulate, while gains from finishing early do not. This is because when an activity is late, those that must wait for it to be completed start later than scheduled. On the other hand, if an activity should be finished before it was scheduled to finish, the advantage rarely can be used, because in complicated projects different crews and materials have to be gathered, and many different people need to be coordinated. The early finish time is not usually known much prior to the activity's completion. Therefore, it is very difficult to gather all of the following activities' resources together in time to start early.

Once the final planned time schedule is developed, it can be used to estimate costs, such as expenditures for human resources, materials, and overhead. The time resources are required is a major component of estimated cost. Also important are materials used, as well as vendor-delivered products. Overhead expenses can be estimated independently of work volume. Obviously, since time is a major element in estimating budgets, one of the major reasons projects run over budget is because they take more time than expected.

Project managers usually focus on scheduling the critical chain of activities closely, to make sure that they have the resources needed to proceed as scheduled. The critical chain of activities includes those activities that are critical (as long as managerial control can influence their duration), but is not limited to these activities. Activities with very little slack can become problems if they are delayed up to or beyond their slack. Therefore, the slack of noncritical activities should also be monitored, to make sure that new critical activities are identified.

Buffers

The primary means to ensure that critical activities are completed on time is to use buffers. A buffer is time that is included in the schedule to protect against unanticipated delays, and to allow early starts. Buffers are different from slack. Slack is spare time. Buffers are time blocks that are not expected to be used for work time (the same as slack), but are dedicated to cover most likely contingencies, and are closely watched so that if they are not needed, subsequent activities can proceed at the earliest time possible. **Project buffers** are used after the final task of a project to protect project completion time from delays. **Feeding buffers** are placed at each point where a noncritical activity is related to a critical path activity. Feeding buffers protect the critical activities from tasks that precede them, and allow for early starts of critical activities. **Resource buffers** are placed before resources that are scheduled to work on critical activities to ensure that resources will be available and that their shortage will not delay critical activities. Resource buffers can be implemented by either issuing warning notices to those managing the resource ahead of the required time, or scheduling a time to mobilize the resource as a predecessor to the critical activity using it. In multiple-project environments, **strategic resource buffers** can be used to ensure that key resources are available for critical activities.

To demonstrate the use of buffers, consider the advertising schedule presented in this section. If the campaign had to be completed in eight weeks, there is currently no room for a project buffer, as the chain of critical activities (activities A–B–C–E) have a planned duration of eight weeks, equal to the available time. However, there may be ways to accomplish specific tasks at the cost of some extra effort or expenditure. For instance, it may be possible to obtain the product manager's approval in one week rather than the planned three weeks. This is an attractive activity to shorten, because it occurs early in the project, and if approval is not obtained, effort on later activities will not be wasted. The product manager may require a thorough analysis. If this thorough analysis is accomplished by working late hours during the week and working weekends, it may be possible to develop the required analysis within a week. This would allow shortening the project by two weeks, as shown in the schedule shown in Figure 7.4.

There now are two weeks available before the project needs to be completed. One of these weeks can be used as a project buffer, insulating the work that needs to be done from the project deadline. (This leaves one additional week of slack for each activity, making no activities critical at this point.) Project buffer is not planned to be used, but is available should something go wrong with critical activities, or with noncritical activities beyond their available slack.

		W	E	E	K	S			
Activity	Duration	1	2	3	4	5	6	7	8
A rough design of advertising plan	1 week	▓						b	s
B convince product manager to adopt	1 week		▓					b	s
C develop marketing plan with staff	3 weeks			▓	▓	▓		b	s
D identify media alternatives	2 weeks			▓	▓	s		b	s
E print materials	1 week						▓	b	s
F brief sales force	2 weeks			▓	▓	s	s	b	s
G select media	1 week					▓	s	b	s
	Scheduled	▓							
	Slack	s							
	BUFFER	b							

Figure 7.4 Demonstration of buffer

Feeding buffers can be used as pseudo-activities to marshal required resources, making sure that they are available in time and that critical activities are not delayed. For instance, activity E, printing materials, is crucial. The marketing plan must be completed before printing can begin, because the marketing plan is the essence of what is to be produced. The project manager can plan on using week 6 as a buffer to ensure that all materials needed by the printer are available (Figure 7.5).

Now the critical activities reappear. Critical activities are activities without slack. All seven activities have a week of project buffer in week 8. Activity E has a week of feeding buffer in week 6, when materials are gathered to ensure that the critical printing activity will proceed as planned. There is now no slack for the chain A–B–C–E. An equivalent way to model this schedule is shown in Figure 7.6.

The critical path would now be A–B–C–CE–E. It is important that if the buffer is not needed, subsequent activities should proceed to work early. For instance, if the feeding buffer between activities C and E is not required, and all required material is ready at the beginning of week 6, printing should go ahead in week 6. If the duration of activity E is the

		W	E	E	K	S			
Activity	Duration	1	2	3	4	5	6	7	8
A rough design of advertising plan	1 week	█							b
B convince product manager to adopt	1 week		█						b
C develop marketing plan with staff	3 weeks			█	█	█			b
D identify media alternatives	2 weeks			█	█	s			b
E print materials	1 week						b	█	b
F brief sales force	2 weeks				█	s	s		b
G select media	1 week					█	s		b
	Scheduled	█							
	Slack	s							
	BUFFER	b							

Figure 7.5 Advertising schedule critical path

		W	E	E	K	S			
Activity	Duration	1	2	3	4	5	6	7	8
A rough design of advertising plan	1 week	█							b
B convince product manager to adopt	1 week		█						b
C develop marketing plan with staff	3 weeks			█	█	█			b
D identify media alternatives	2 weeks			█	█	s			b
CE feeding buffer	1 week						b		
E print materials	1 week							█	b
F brief sales force	2 weeks				█	s	s		b
G select media	1 week					█	s		b
	Scheduled	█							
	Slack	s							
	Critical	█	b						
	BUFFER	b							

Figure 7.6 Equivalent model using feeding buffer

planned one week, the project would then be completed by the end of week 6. If the feeding buffer CE turns out to be needed, and printing require extra time, there is project buffer available in week 8. This buffer, like all other buffers, should not be used unless necessary in light of sound management principles.

Resource buffers could be used if a key resource, such as the team that develops the advertising plan, were heavily scheduled on other activities. A resource buffer in that case would be time allocated to ensure that the key resource had time to gear up for this particular project. In construction, an obvious resource buffer could exist if there were a key piece of equipment, such as a large crane, that was very expensive and valuable for many other projects. (In this case, it would be a strategic resource buffer.) The key resource might be needed elsewhere, or might be found to be across the country working on a prior project. A strategic resource buffer would then be included in the schedule to ensure that time was available to transport it, to replace it if necessary (and possible), or in case of mechanical difficulties, to repair it. The resource buffer, like all four forms of buffer, represents planning ahead for reasonable contingencies.

Project Crashing

Another possibility is that extra resources can be acquired to complete critical activities quicker. This creates a problem for management, trading off quicker completion time with higher cost. If the savings from faster completion time are known, then the problem is simply one of minimizing cost. Often, however, it is a matter of risk, in that you know some activities are subject to delay, and earlier planned finishing times are far safer than those plans that push things to some deadline.

To demonstrate crashing, consider a problem of importing some critical piece of equipment from Australia, which you have contracted to install for a client. Figure 7.7 gives a network for this project. You have agreed to get the equipment installed and running in 12 days. If you are late, you will pay a penalty of $500 per day for each day beyond the contracted 12 days.

The critical path calculations for the basic model are shown in Table 7.7.

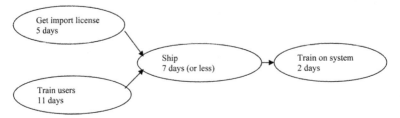

Figure 7.7 *Network for delivery from Australia*

Table 7.7 *Slack calculations*

Activity	Duration	Pred	Early Start	Early Finish	Late Start	Late Finish	Slack
A Get import license	5 days	None	0	5	0	5	0
B Ship	7 days	A	5	12	5	12	0
C Train Users	11 days	None	0	11	1	12	1
D Train on System	2 days	B, C	12	14	12	14	0

Figure 7.8 displays the schedule for the base case.

The critical path, which takes 14 days, is A–B–D. Activity C has one day of slack. But this plan involves a penalty of $1,000, because it is two days late. The options available for activity B ship are shown in Table 7.8:

The base plan uses the least cost method, the slow boat. However, it incurs penalties of $1,000. Clearly it would be cost effective to adopt a faster delivery method. Crashing analyzes this cost tradeoff.

The crashing procedure is to identify the least cost method of reducing duration of activities on the critical path one time unit at a time. The critical path here is A–B–D. Actually, in this problem, there is only one activity that can be accomplished faster than the original schedule—activity B. The next least cost method is a fast boat, which costs $300 rather than the slow boat cost of $100, for a marginal added cost of $200. This would reduce the duration of activity B to 6, resulting in the following critical path schedule (Table 7.9).

		D	A	Y	S										
Activity	Duration	1	2	3	4	5	6	7	8	9	10	11	12	13	14
A license	5 d	■	■	■	■	■									
B slow boat	7 d						■	■	■	■	■	■	■		
C train users	11 d	▨	▨	▨	▨	▨	▨	▨	▨	▨	▨	▨	s		
D train on system	2 d													■	■
	Scheduled	▨													
	Slack	s													
	Critical	■													

Figure 7.8 Australian delivery schedule

Table 7.8 Logistics options

Option	Time (Days)	Cost	
Slow boat	7	$100	The base option
Fast boat	6	$300	
Bush airplane	5	$400	
Normal airplane	3	$500	
Chartered plane	1	$900	

Table 7.9 Revised schedule

Activity	Duration	Pred	Early Start	Early Finish	Late Start	Late Finish	Slack
A Get import license	5 days	None	0	5	0	5	0
B Ship	6 days	A	5	11	5	11	0
C Train Users	11 days	None	0	11	0	11	0
D Train on System	2 days	B, C	11	13	11	13	0

		D	A	Y	S									
Activity	Duration	1	2	3	4	5	6	7	8	9	10	11	12	13
A license	5 d													
B slow boat	6 d													
C train users	11 d													
D train on system	2 d													
	Scheduled													
	Slack	s												
	Critical													

Figure 7.9 Revised schedule

The schedule for this revision is shown in Figure 7.9.

This new schedule saves $500 in penalties, at an added cost of $200, for a net savings of $300. This clearly is superior to the original schedule. The difference between this schedule and the original schedule is that activity B has been crashed one day. Another result is that now all four activities are critical (all have zero slack). From looking at the network, we can see that there are now two critical paths: A–B–D and C–D. This means that if we want to reduce the project completion time, we will have to shorten both critical paths in parallel. While it is possible to reduce the original critical path A–B–D by adopting the bush airplane option, this will do nothing to reduce the new critical path, C–D. Therefore, there are no savings in penalties, while there is an added cost of $100 by moving from the fast boat to the bush plane. Thus, we would not be interested in further crashing the project, but would adopt the fast boat shipping option.

Crashing also can be applied to identify a cost/time tradeoff. The following example (Table 7.10) demonstrates this concept.

The network for this project is shown in Figure 7.10.

The schedule is shown in Figure 7.11.

The original critical path model requires 58 days to complete. This is with no extra costs for crashing.

Table 7.10 Second crashing project

Activity	Duration (Days)	Pred	Early Start	Early Finish	Late Start	Late Finish	Slack	Crash
A Develop layout	19	none	0	19	0	19	0	
B Obtain permits	5	A	19	24	19	24	0	10,000/ day 1 max
C Facility work	30	B	24	54	24	54	0	3,000/ day 1 max
D Inspect cabling	2	C	54	56	54	56	0	
E Install remote lines	53	None	0	53	1	54	1	5,000/ day 12 max
F Test lines	2	E	53	55	54	56	1	
G Test system	2	D, F	56	58	56	58	0	

The next step is to identify critical activities that can be crashed. If more than one critical path exists, all critical paths must be reduced the same amount. In our case, there is one critical path: A-B-C-D-G. Of these critical activities, B and C can be crashed. The least expensive would be selected. In this case, that is C (at $3,000/day as opposed to $10,000/day for B).

By crashing C one day at a cost of $3,000, we can complete the project in 57 days (see Table 7.11).

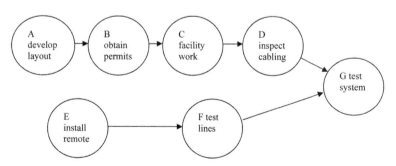

Figure 7.10 Network for line project

		D	A	Y	S														
Activity	Duration	1	2	3	4	..	10	..	19	20	..	24	25	..	53	54	55	56	57	58
A	19 d					..		..											
B	5 d																		
C	30 d													..					
D	2 d																		
E	53 d					..		..				..			..	s				
F	2 d															s			
G	2 d																		
	Scheduled																		
	Slack	S																	
	Critical																		

Figure 7.11 Schedule for second crashing example

Table 7.11 Second crashing project after crashing C

Activity	Duration	Pred	Early Start	Early Finish	Late Start	Late Finish	Slack	Crash
A Develop layout	19 days	none	0	19	0	19	0	
B Obtain permits	5 days	A	19	24	19	24	0	10,000/ day 1 max
C Facility work	29 days	B	24	53	24	53	0	
D Inspect cabling	2 days	C	53	55	53	55	0	
E Install remote lines	53 days	None	0	53	0	53	0	5,000/day 12 max
F Test lines	2 days	E	53	55	53	55	0	
G Test system	2 days	D, F	55	57	55	57	0	

The schedule after crashing activity C is shown in Figure 7.12.

Now there are two critical paths: A–B–C–D–G and E–F–G. On the first path, our choices for crashing are B and C, with C still the least cost option at $3,000/day. On the second critical path, the only activity that can be crashed is E, at a cost of $5,000/day. If G had been crashable, it would have served for both critical paths, because it is an element of both.

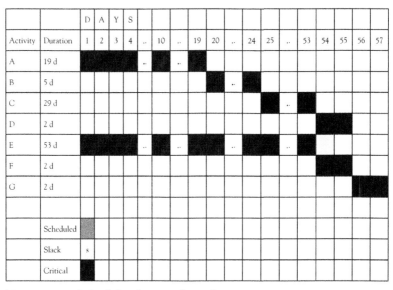

Figure 7.12 Schedule after crashing C

However, if G is not available (and it is not), we must crash two activities, in this case C and E at a total cost of $8,000. This yields a solution
(Table 7.12) completing the project in 56 days at an added cumulative
cost of $11,000 (including the $3,000 spent to get to 57 days).

Table 7.12 Second crashing project after crashing C and E

Activity	Duration	Pred	Early Start	Early Finish	Late Start	Late Finish	Slack	Crash
A Develop layout	19 days	none	0	19	0	19	0	
B Obtain permits	5 days	A	19	24	19	24	0	10,000/day 1 max
C Facility work	28 days	B	24	52	24	52	0	
D Inspect cabling	2 days	C	52	54	52	54	0	
E Install remote lines	52 days	None	0	52	0	52	0	5,000/day 11 max
F Test lines	2 days	E	52	54	52	54	0	
G Test system	2 days	D, F	54	56	54	56	0	

Table 7.13 Third crashing project after crashing B, C, and E twice

Activity	Duration	Pred	Early Start	Early Finish	Late Start	Late Finish	Slack	Crash
A Develop layout	19 days	None	0	19	0	19	0	
B Obtain permits	4 days	A	19	23	19	23	0	
C Facility work	28 days	B	23	51	23	51	0	
D Inspect cabling	2 days	C	51	53	51	53	0	
E Install remote lines	51 days	None	0	51	0	51	0	5,000/day 10 max
F Test lines	2 days	E	51	53	51	53	0	
G Test system	2 days	D, F	53	55	53	55	0	

We have trimmed both critical paths. All activities remain critical, and there are two critical paths: A–B–C–D–G and E–F–G. We have now exhausted the days we can crash on activity C, so our only option is now to reduce activity B to 4 days by spending another $10,000, at the same time that we reduce activity E to 51 days at an added cost of $5,000. This would reduce the project duration to 55 days (Table 7.13), at a cumulative cost of $26,000.

At this stage, we can no longer reduce the duration of the critical path chain A–B–C–D–G, and so we must stop. The table of tradeoffs resulting from our analysis is given in Table 7.14.

In this case, we do not have a benefit given for saving a day of project time. This often is the case. Managers are provided with the expected cost for a given project duration. Managers seeking the lowest expected cost would risk the 58-day plan. More cautious managers may want to spend the extra money to save time, or to increase the cushion for project completion.

Table 7.14 Crashing options

Original schedule	58 days	No extra expenditure
Crash C 1 day	57 days	$3,000 extra cost
Crash C 1 day, E 1 day	56 days	$11,000 extra cost
Crash B 1 day, C 1 day, E 2 days	55 days	$26,000 extra cost

Resource Leveling

The critical path model we have considered so far has assumed unlimited resources. **Resource leveling** is the process of spreading out the early start schedule, so that the maximum number of a particular resource required can be reduced. For instance, if a particular specialist is needed to accomplish more than one activity, and these activities happen to be scheduled during common periods of time, something would have to give. One or the other of the activities sharing the common resource would have to be delayed (or additional resource acquired).

To demonstrate, consider a project (network in Figure 7.13) with the following data:

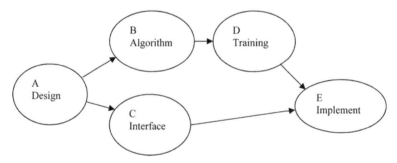

Figure 7.13 Network for leveling project

The project data are given in Table 7.15.

Figure 7.14 gives the schedule for this project.

If the same specialist was required for both activities B and C, they could not be accomplished concurrently. This means that the original critical path model is infeasible. Either B or C must be delayed. The decision of what to delay is a difficult question if you are after the guaranteed

Table 7.15 Leveling project data

Activity	Duration (Weeks)	Pred	Early Start	Early Finish	Late Start	Late Finish	Slack	Resource
A Design	3	None	0	3	0	3	0	
B Algorithm	5	A	3	8	3	8	0	Specialist
C Interface	6	A	3	9	6	12	3	Specialist
D Training	4	B	8	12	8	12	0	
E Implement	3	C, D	12	15	12	15	0	

		W	E	E	K	S										
Activity	Duration	1	2	3	4	5	6	7	8	9	10	11	12	13	14	15
A design	3 w	■	■	■												
B algorithm	5 w				■	■	■	■	■							
C interface	6 w				▨	▨	▨	▨	▨	▨	s	s	s			
D training	4 w									■	■	■	■			
E implement	3 w													■	■	■
	Scheduled	▨														
	Slack	s														
	Critical	■														

Figure 7.14 Schedule for leveling project

Table 7.16 Leveled project after B delayed

Activity	Duration	Pred	Start	Finish	Slack	Resource
A Design	3 weeks	None	0	3	0	
B Algorithm	5 weeks	A	9	14	0	Specialist
C Interface	6 weeks	A	3	9	0	Specialist
D Training	4 weeks	B	14	18	0	
E Implement	3 weeks	C, D	18	21	0	

best answer. For small projects, you might as well check all of the possibilities. For instance, in this case there are only two activities to delay. If B is delayed, it cannot start until week 10, when both activity A is completed and the specialist is through with activity C (Table 7.16).

Figure 7.15 gives the leveled schedule for this project.

In this case, nothing is slack, because delaying any activity will delay the end of the project. We can see this, although the method of using only predecessors will not yield that result, because of the need to consider the limitation on the number of specialists.

The alternative is to delay activity C. This yields Table 7.17.

In this case, activity D will have a slack of 2. The total project is completed in 17 weeks instead of the 21 weeks obtained by delaying activity B (see Figure 7.16). This is still a significant delay, as the original critical path schedule required only 15 weeks.

Activity	Duration	w	e	e	k	s															
		1	2	3	4	5	6	7	8	9	10	11	12	13	14	15	16	17	18	19	20	21
A design	3 w	■	■	■																		
B algorithm	5 w									x	x	x	x	x								
C interface	6 w				x	x	x	x	x	x												
D training	4 w														■	■	■	■				
E implement	3 w																		■	■	■	
	Specialist	x																				

Figure 7.15 Leveled project

Table 7.17 Leveled project after B delayed

Activity	Duration (Weeks)	Pred	Start	Finish	Slack	Resource
A Design	3	None	0	3	0	
B Algorithm	5	A	3	8	0	Specialist
C Interface	6	A	8	14	0	Specialist
D Training	4	B	8	12	2	
E Implement	3	C, D	14	17	0	

Activity	Duration	w	e	e	k	s												
		1	2	3	4	5	6	7	8	9	10	11	12	13	14	15	16	17
A design	3 w	■	■	■														
B algorithm	5 w				x	x	x	x	x									
C interface	6 w									x	x	x	x	x	x			
D training	4 w								■	■	■	■		s	s			
E implement	3 w															■	■	■
	specialist	x																

Figure 7.16 Alternative leveled project

Although there is no guaranteed best way of deciding which activity to delay when sharing scarce resources, it usually works well to use a priority system. A good choice would be to schedule critical activities first, and if more than one critical activity shares the scarce resource, a second priority that is often used is to schedule the longest activity among those selected by the first priority. If multiple resources are limited, an alternative priority could be given to scheduling the resource with the greatest number of limited resources. Project management software usually levels projects for you. They vary in what priority rules they use.

Resource Smoothing

Resource leveling focuses on extending schedules, so that particular resources are not overscheduled. **Resource smoothing** focuses on adjusting schedules to obtain a level amount of work for a given resource. This includes possible extension (or compression) of activities to make work volume more even. It also can include identifying gaps in the work schedule that management might be able to fill by finding extra work.

Consider a multiple-project operation in the information technology industry (Figure 7.17). Four resources are involved: crews for design, for production, for testing, and for installation of information technology products. For simplification, assume that these four activities are accomplished in sequence in the order given. The firm currently has three projects, all with a deadline of being completed by the end of week 20.

Project data are displayed in Table 7.18.

The Gantt chart for this schedule is shown in Figure 7.18.

Usages for each resource are given in Figure 7.19, with a shaded box indicating the total count of each resource required by week. For instance, one design crew is required in weeks 1 through 8, and none thereafter.

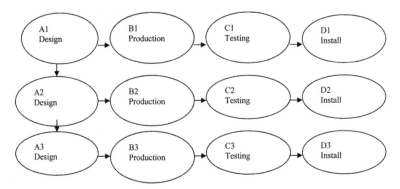

Figure 7.17 Network for smoothing projects

Table 7.18 Multiple-project operation

Activity	Duration (Weeks)	Predecessor	Start	Finish	Resource
A1 Design	2	None	0	2	Design crew
B1 Production	4	A1	2	6	Production crew
C1 Test	2	B1	6	8	Testing crew
D1 Install	1	C1	8	9	Installation crew
A2 Design	2s	A1	2	4	Design crew
B2 Production	5	A2	4	9	Production crew
C2 Test	3	B2	9	12	Testing crew
D2 Install	1	C2	12	13	Installation crew
A3 Design	4	A2	4	8	Design crew
B3 Production	6	A3	8	14	Production crew
C3 Test	3	B3	14	17	Testing crew
D3 Install	1	C3	17	18	Installation crew

One production crew is needed in weeks 3 and 4, and two production crews needed in weeks 5 and 6.

A smooth schedule is one where a resource is working the same level of activity each time period. These resource usage charts indicate that

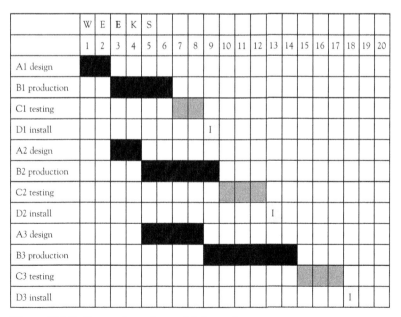

Figure 7.18 Gantt chart for multiple projects

there are two types of smoothing that might be useful: gaps in work to do, and excess work to do. When there is no work to do, a valley (no activity) is encountered. When there is too much work scheduled for a period, a peak occurs. There are valleys for the testing and installation crews. The only peaks occur for the production crew.

For all four crews, slack resources exist in that there are periods where no work is currently scheduled. This is because greater resource capacity exists than work required. Some spare resources are required to cover the inevitable uncertainty in projects. Efficiency, on the other hand, seeks to utilize all

Design	W	E	E	K	S															
	1	2	3	4	5	6	7	8	9	10	11	12	13	14	15	16	17	18	19	20
# crews needed:																				
Two																				
One		■	■	■	■	■	■	■												

Production	W	E	E	K	S															
	1	2	3	4	5	6	7	8	9	10	11	12	13	14	15	16	17	18	19	20
# crews needed:																				
Two				■	■	■		■	■											
One			■	■	■	■	■	■	■	■	■	■	■							

Testing	W	E	E	K	S															
	1	2	3	4	5	6	7	8	9	10	11	12	13	14	15	16	17	18	19	20
# crews needed:																				
Two																				
One								▓	▓		▓	▓	▓			▓	▓			

Install	W	E	E	K	S															
	1	2	3	4	5	6	7	8	9	10	11	12	13	14	15	16	17	18	19	20
# crews needed:																				
Two																				
One									I				I				I			

Figure 7.19 Resource usage by crew

resources at their capacity at all times. Being careful to assure that important project activities are not delayed for lack of resource, management may be able to increase efficiency by finding useful activities for resources during their unscheduled periods (or laying off crews when no work is to be done). One approach is investment in training and development activities. Another approach is to find more work. However, it is apparent here that there is also an imbalance across resources. If management were to obtain more work similar to that they have, the production crew would fall further and further behind, because their work per project is always longest. The gaps for the testing crew, and especially for the installation crew, would get wider and wider. Sound management practice here calls for balancing, through hiring additional production crews. If a great deal of similar work is obtained, more analysis crews might be called for as well. As a simple fix to this operation's problem, we add a second production crew to accomplish production work on the second project in Figure 7.20.

The schedules for each of the production crews now are smoothed in the sense that they are not overscheduled (Figure 7.21).

However, there is obviously more waste time that management needs to fill.

	W	E	E	K	S															
	1	2	3	4	5	6	7	8	9	10	11	12	13	14	15	16	17	18	19	20
A1 design	■	■																		
B1 production			■	■	■															
C1 testing						▨	▨													
D1 install								1												
A2 design			■																	
B2 production					2	2	2	2	2											
C2 testing										▨	▨									
D2 install													1							
A3 design					x	x	x	x												
B3 production									1	1	1	1	1	1						
C3 testing															▨	▨	▨			
D3 install																		1		

Figure 7.20 Schedule with second production crew

Production 1	W	E	E	K	S															
	1	2	3	4	5	6	7	8	9	10	11	12	13	14	15	16	17	18	19	20
# crews needed																				
Two																				
One			1	1	1	1			1	1	1	1	1	1						

Production 2	W	E	E	K	S															
	1	2	3	4	5	6	7	8	9	10	11	12	13	14	15	16	17	18	19	20
# crews needed																				
Two																				
One					2	2	2	2	2											

Figure 7.21 Smoothed production crews

The second smoothing condition is to lower the peak workloads. This requires either delaying the schedule, or hiring additional resources (demonstrated in the last section). Delaying the schedule (returning to the case using one production crew) can eliminate the excess workload (Figure 7.22).

	W	E	E	K	S															
	1	2	3	4	5	6	7	8	9	10	11	12	13	14	15	16	17	18	19	20
A1 design	x	x																		
B1 production			1	1	1	1														
C1 testing							x	x												
D1 install								x												
A2 design			x	x																
B2 production							2	2	2	2	2									
C2 testing												x	x	x						
D2 install														x						
A3 design					x	x	x	x												
B3 production													1	1	1	1	1	1		
C3 testing																		x	x	x
D3 install																				

Figure 7.22 Delayed (smoothed) schedule

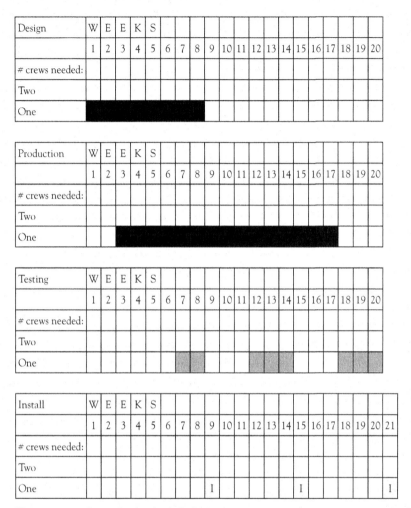

Figure 7.23 Smoothed schedule by crews

However, eliminating the overscheduling entirely using existing resources would require extending the last project into week 21. The resource usages would now be as shown in Figure 7.23.

Smoothing is a managerial decision. The ideal would involve balancing crew capacities so that each crew could work the same amount each time period. That is what assembly line operations do. That requires a highly predictable environment, which simply does not exist in projects. Projects will inevitably experience gaps in work, along with some periods of critical resource shortage. The quality of project management can be measured on a scale of efficiency by the proportion of waste time encountered. However, priority should be given to ensuring that critical activities have the resources they need, even if it involves some waste. It is more important to get the job done right, on time, and within budget, than to obtain a perfectly smooth schedule.

Critical Path Criticisms

Like any model, the critical path approach makes a number of assumptions. Usually, the more convenient the assumptions are for mathematical solution, the less realistic the assumptions are relative to the real decision. The critical path model as demonstrated above is very useful in identifying the fastest one can expect to complete a project. But we have seen in prior chapters that things rarely proceed as planned, and in practice the original critical path plan usually requires significant modification as the project proceeds and more accurate activity durations are obtained. There is usually significant variance in possible durations of activities, with options available to speed selected activities. Crashing provides one means of obtaining greater understanding for these situations. One approach to uncertainty is to focus on scheduling milestones. Uncertainty in activity durations is addressed by PERT models and simulation, but those get involved. Another key idea is that the critical path includes those activities that should be most closely managed. Critical activities are important to monitor closely. But those activities with apparent slack can become critical, and should not be ignored.

The critical path model assumes unlimited resources. We have discussed leveling as a means of analyzing the effects of limited resources. An additional extension of this concept is smoothing. Projects typically involve highly variable workloads, with employment starting at a very low volume, jumping to high levels in the middle of the project, and then in general declining. This overall trend masks even greater variations for the workload of specific skill sets, which can be highly erratic. Smoothing seeks to level the workload of the project, sacrificing minimum time for a more even workload. In information system projects this is less important, as the usual condition is many projects going on at once, with more than enough work for individuals on other projects as soon as their work on this project is completed. The matrix form of organization, discussed in Chapter 3, is highly appropriate for this environment, allowing individuals to be shuffled into a particular project to perform their specialty, and then moving on to the next project requiring their services.

The critical path model assumes that activities can be addressed as entities, with clear beginning and ending points. In reality, the content of complex projects changes over time. As new events unfold, project progress may require change in direction. An obvious impact relative to information systems projects is the outcome of testing. According to plan, testing will find that everything was successfully built as scheduled. In reality, the outcome of testing is highly uncertain. There is a possibility that testing will find that the system components do perform as designed. If they don't, however, new activities will be required: to identify the cause of the problem, to decide how to revise the system, and quite possibly to build new system components.

Summary

The critical path method provides project managers with valuable information. The criticality of project activities can be identified, and those activities that are critical can be managed more closely. The critical path method provides an estimate of how long the project will take if everything takes no longer than estimated. The critical path method displays what can happen due to predecessor relationships. Crashing provides a means of comparing the tradeoff in cost and time in project scheduling. However, the critical path method assumes unlimited resources, which may not be realistic.

There are some things managers can do when facing resource limits. Buffers provide a way to better manage the chain of critical activities. Most project management software systems allow managers to level resources, generally following a priority system as we have outlined. While not guaranteed to give the best solution, this ability of software packages to level resources is extremely useful.

Projects can also be leveled to stay within available resources, and even smoothed to more efficiently schedule resources. Project management software is very good at accomplishing the task of leveling project activities to stay within prescribed resource levels. The solutions provided are not necessarily the best possible, but are usually very good. The activity of smoothing is not as critical in project management, because efficiency is not as important as dealing with the high levels of uncertainty present in projects. Smoothing in uncertain environments is usually not effective.

A recent research article on critical chain project scheduling in referenced.[1]

Glossary

Buffers: Time built into a schedule to allow for anticipated contingencies.

Crashing: Compressing an activity duration at a cost.

Critical activity: Activity with zero scheduling slack.

Critical path: Chain of activities with zero slack that must be completed on time for the project to meet its scheduled completion time.

Early start schedule: Schedule designed to accomplish each task as early as possible.

Feeding buffers: Buffers added to a project to protect the task in question from delays in completion of predecessor activities.

Float: Synonym for slack.

Gantt chart: Bar chart of project tasks plotted against time units.

Independent slack: Slack not shared with other tasks.

Late start schedule: Schedule designed to accomplish each task as late as possible while maintaining expected project completion time.

Network: Sketch showing the predecessor relationships among project tasks.

Project buffers: Buffers added to a project after its final task to ensure against delay in project completion time.

Resource buffers: Buffers added to a project before a task to ensure that the resources it requires are available.

Resource leveling: Adjusting a critical path schedule to avoid overuse of limited resources.

Resource smoothing: Adjusting a schedule to make the use of resources more uniform, minimizing resource usage peaks and valleys.

Shared slack: Slack that is common to two tasks (if one of these tasks were to be late, it would exhaust its own slack, as well as the slack of the sharing task).

Slack: Extra time available to accomplish a task beyond the time scheduled, while still allowing the project to be completed as scheduled.

Strategic resource buffers: Buffers added to projects in multiple-project environments to ensure that key resources are available for critical activities.

PMBOK Items Relating to Chapter 7:

6.1 Plan Schedule Management—process of establishing the policies, procedures, and documentation for planning, developing, managing, executing, and controlling the project schedule.

6.2 Define Activities—process of identifying and documenting the specific actions to be performed to produce the project deliverables.

6.3 Sequence Activities—process of identifying and documenting relationships among the project activities.

6.6 Develop Schedule—process of analyzing activity sequences, durations, resource requirements, and schedule constraints to create the project schedule model.

Reference

1   W. Peng and M. Huang. 2014. "A Critical Chain Project Scheduling Method Based on a Differential Evolution Algorithm," *International Journal of Production Research* 52, no. 13, pp. 3940–3949.

PART IV

Project Completion

CHAPTER 8

Project Control and Assessment

Project control, like risk analysis and estimation, needs to be applied from the beginning of the project to the project's end. **Control** is concerned with keeping the project on target with respect to its objectives. Assessment is the means of monitoring project progress to identify problems requiring control action. The project, to be a success, should conform to the project plan as much as possible. Project management must adapt to new circumstances while simultaneously seeking to meet cost, time, and quality targets. This requires close coordination between the project manager and his or her superiors, whether they are part of the same organization or not.

Risk Management

We have seen that there are many potential problems that need to be anticipated in project management. There are many risks in software development projects. The actions to alleviate these risks are means of control. Actions need to be taken throughout the project, to include continual monitoring to ensure that problems do not get out of control.

Personnel Shortfalls

In the area of personnel management, one obvious approach is to obtain quality people. When operating in a matrix organization, people are obtained from the functional areas of the organization. Boehm recommended meeting with these functional managers to pre-schedule good people by name, and documenting these agreements. If people are obtained either from a matrix organization or from outside the organization, references should be checked to improve the probability that they will fit their planned roles.

The second personnel technique is team building. Proactive efforts should be taken to see that project management and team members share objectives. Participative planning and objective setting activities are useful to attain this aim, as well as group consensus techniques. Brainstorming, the Nominal Group Technique, and Delphi methods are tools that can lead to group consensus by sharing ideas on the issue under consideration.

Controlling Dynamic Requirements

Project requirements sometimes are changed extensively. Some change needs to be accommodated, as there are inevitable environmental changes that must be adjusted for. We have stressed user involvement. But once the scope of the project has been set, additional change (what systems people call scope creep) can be very detrimental to productivity. Some projects get out of control in the sense that requirements are constantly adjusted. One response to gain control over such a situation is to have a **high change threshold**, not changing plans until it is absolutely clear that they are needed. Risks are also reduced by deferring development of those project components that involve high probabilities of change. Another means of dealing with inevitable changes consists of determining major directions of anticipated changes in requirements, and developing the system, so that only minor revisions to the system are required (only one module would need to be replaced rather than revising the entire system).

Controlling Externally Provided Project Components

Combining system components obtained from multiple sources always creates risks of compatibility. These risks can be reduced by the activities of coordination and inspection. **Reference checking** involves contacting existing users of the component in question to verify features such as ease of use, ease of change, and other critical risk factors. **Pre-award audits** in the form of checklists and other techniques can be used to reduce the risk that outside vendors are incapable of delivering the component they are to provide. Other means of reducing the risk of failure in externally furnished components include use of award-fee contracts, soliciting competitive designs and prototypes, and involving outside providers in the project team.

Real-Time Performance Risk

The ability of the developed system to perform under actual working conditions is always uncertain until the system is implemented. There are a number of techniques available to reduce the risk of inadequate performance. In the context of project management, **benchmarking** involves placing the system under a representative workload and analyzing the system's ability to cope with this level of activity. Prototyping is another means of testing the critical performance features of a system. Instrumentation and tuning measure system performance in terms of bottlenecks. When bottlenecks are encountered, workload can be adjusted by changing task sequence, priorities, data distribution, and other workload characteristics to improve system performance. **Technical analysis** examines the ability of the system to function in environments such as distributed processing. The system's fault tolerance, security, and accuracy are also tested. Techniques supporting technical analysis include fault-tree analysis, and failure modes and effects analysis.

Contingent Development Methods

Software systems should deliver functions needed by users. **Incremental development** allows organizations to test the functionality of system parts without wasting money on the entire project should it prove inadequate. **Prototyping** is a useful means of verifying the functionality of systems to users. Prototyping is also good for assessing the fault tolerance of systems. As the functionality of systems components is evaluated, those that are found lacking can be eliminated by **requirements scrubbing**. Cost-benefit methods provide one basis for deciding on whether to keep a system feature or not.

Mission analysis is the process of evaluating the contribution of a system component to accomplish an organizational objective. Mission analysis requires examination of the user's mission, and the role of information system support in leading to successful accomplishment of those missions. One of the key factors in information system project success has been identified as clear statement of project objectives. Mission analysis would be a way of implementing this key factor. Tools to study the user's mission include identification of user tasks, data flows, and control procedures, as well as cost-benefit analysis.

Unrealistic Estimates

Many projects suffer from difficulties in obtaining accurate estimates of cost and time in information systems projects. One approach is to design projects to the available budget. The level of delivered functionality would be a variable. Software system components could be prioritized into mandatory, desired, and optional groups. The final design would have to include mandatory items, should include desired items, and would include optional items only if adequate time and budget were available.

The Control Process

There are some fundamental differences between planning and control. Planning focuses on setting goals and directions. Control is interested in guiding project effort toward attainment of these goals. Planning involves allocating resources to elements of the project hierarchy. Control seeks to ensure effective use of these resources. Planning requires anticipation of problems. Control requires correction of problems. Planning is a motivational effort, while control is more a matter of rewarding achievement.

Control requires understanding what is going on with a project. Project managers need to visit operations, and see for themselves what is going on. Many actual problems do not show up in reports until too late for effective corrective action to be taken. Furthermore, a sense of the morale of members of the project team is better gained by actual visits.

Visits, in turn, do not reveal details about performance that reports can. Reports of project progress should be as accurate as possible. Reports are used in a control sense by providing concrete measures of actual versus planned accomplishments of technical activities. Both time and cost reports are crucial to give the project manager a clear picture of project performance. Major variances need to be understood by the project manager. There could be reasons beyond the control of anyone connected with the project. On the other hand, they could be the result of things that the project management team could correct. These variances also trigger a need for overall management to decide whether the project should be continued or dropped.

There are three general phases of the control process. **Performance standards** are set at the beginning of the project. These provide technical specifications, budgeted costs, schedules, and resource requirements. Source documents include user specifications and the project plan. Comparisons are made between actual performance and the plan during operations (**assessment**). Major project control elements include projected completion date and total estimated project cost. When severe variances are experienced, the adoption of **corrective action** needs to be considered.

Control Process

Performance Standards
Assessment
Corrective Action

There are many tools to control project development. We review three representatives here, in the area of personnel management, accounting, and work authorization.

Responsibility Assignment

A project team is formed to bring people with a variety of skills together to accomplish the project's objectives. A project responsibility chart is a simple device commonly used to clearly state who is responsible for each project activity (Figure 8.1).

Activities: Develop Project Plan	User	PM	CE	SA	PT
A1 Initial project plan	A	I		X	
A2 Detailed plan of system modules				X	C
A3 Revise overall project plan	d	d			
A4 Complete resource, time, and cost estimates			P	X	C
A5 Review	d	d	C	C	C
A6 Final plan revision	I	I		X	I

Personnel:		Responsibility:
User	who the system is to be built for	X – executes task
PM	project manager	D – solely responsible for decision
CE	cost estimator	d – shared decision responsibility
SA	systems analyst	P – manages work and controls progress
PT	production team	C – needs to be consulted
		I – needs to be informed
		A – available for advice

Figure 8.1 Example of a responsibility chart

Note that the RACI charts discussed in Chapter 6 are closely related to the responsibility chart given in Figure 8.1. Both forms can be used to clearly delineate the responsibilities of all parties involved. Also valuable is the information related to who must be consulted, informed, or is available for advice.

Budget

The traditional means of implementing cost control is **variance analysis**. Accurate measurement requires accurate identification of the quantities of work involved. Some costs are nonlinear, making it more difficult to estimate costs. This is especially true in information system projects, where progress is uncertain until testing is complete.

Cost control works most effectively when it is tied to work packages. **Work packages** include work descriptions, time-phased budgets, work plans and schedules, resource requirements, and assignments of responsibility. To make sense of cost reports, managers need to keep up with changes, generated by schedule delay, and differences in planned and actual times, changes in the scope of work. The **earned value concept** is very useful to project management in this process. Earned value is the measure of the budgeted value of work that has been accomplished. Earned value indicates how much of the budget was planned to have been spent in order to do the amount of work done so far. This concept operates on the **standard time unit**, which measures work accomplished in terms of what a normal, prudent worker with average luck would accomplish in that time unit. Standard hours are traditionally used in manufacturing. Other time units, such as day or week, can be used as well. A standard week is probably more appropriate for information systems work. This can be useful in measuring the efficiency of a work unit. It also focuses on activity completion. Calculations are shown in Table 8.1.

In this example, work packages A and B are completed, so the earned value is easy to calculate. The measures for unfinished activities are more problematic, because it is difficult to accurately estimate the percentage of work completed. We have seen that in information systems projects, the final testing and debugging phases can include a great deal of unanticipated work. However, estimates of earned values can be calculated. In this case, credit is taken for half of the effort required on activity C, and 75 percent of the effort required on activity D.

Relative efficiency can be calculated by dividing earned hours by actual hours. For instance, if the actual effort expended on work package A was 25, it would have been rated as $20/25 = 0.80$ efficient. If work package B took 8 units of effort, the efficiency rating would be $10/8 = 1.25$, or 25 percent more efficient than expected. If activities C and D had actual expenditures equal to their earned value, the efficiency of this project component as a whole would be the total earned value (51) divided by total expended effort (54) $= 51/54 = 0.94$, or 94 percent of planned, on average. However, these measures need to be considered in

Table 8.1 Earned value calculations

Work Package	Budgeted	% Complete	Earned Value	Actual
A	20	100	20	25
B	10	100	10	8
C	12	50	6	6
D	20	75	15	15
TOTALS			51	54

light of conditions beyond the control of the project team. If late deliveries of materials or software cause work package A to run over its budget, the inefficiency could not in all fairness be attributed to poor performance on the part of those responsible for doing the work of work package A. Project management needs to coordinate closely with the project team to understand the reasons for work lagging in time, or running over in cost.

People have a tendency to do the easiest work first, especially if it is important to appear as if they are making progress. In project environments, this often leads to higher levels of progress reported than is actually the case. Projects are almost always reported to be on schedule until they are about 90 or 95 percent complete. Some activities actually finish as scheduled. But many activities start to lag behind the planned completion date in the latter stages of their work. One reason for this in information systems projects is that problems are often not identified until the testing stage. Progress reports in projects should be considered suspect until actual completion. That is the principal point of the milestone concept.

A primary role of the project information system is to monitor project progress. Data is collected from a variety of sources, including materials invoices, time cards, change notices, test results, and attitude surveys. Reports convey this information to key managers. All levels of management need to be provided the detailed information they need to identify problems and take corrective action. These reports need to identify variances. They also need to be published in a timely fashion.

Work Authorization

Authorization is a primary means of controlling projects. Upper management authorizes the project manager to proceed. The project manager in turn authorizes departments within the project management team to accomplish various elements of work through work orders. The authorization chain works its way down through the organization. Ensuring that expenditure and work activity do not proceed without authorization is a primary means of maintaining control over the project.

The data collection process works pretty much in reverse of the authorization flow. Work sections report their progress to their managers, who report up the hierarchy until ultimately the project manager receives summarized reports. These summary reports need to focus on problems, and to identify accomplishments to date and current cost performance. The project manager needs to keep upper management informed. Upper management usually uses project information to merely keep informed of activities, unless things get so bad that canceling the project appears appropriate.

Because of the uncertain nature of information systems projects, change is to be expected. Management control through work authorization is a way to manage this change. Reasons for change include:

- Change in project scope and specification
- Changes in design
- Changes to improve rate of return
- Changes to adopt improvements

The owner may desire change in project scope and specification due to new circumstances. These can arise because of new regulations, or changes in the market. Changes in design can occur if it is clear that the original plan will not work, or possibly new technology may now be available that is clearly better than what was known when the project was adopted. These can arise due to errors, omissions, afterthoughts, or revised needs. Such changes can offer opportunities for improvement, but may also open up opportunities for major foul-ups. Changes to improve the rate of return are a financial factor, where the owner has better things to do with the money required by the project.

Changes are troublesome for project teams. The more the project is completed, the more difficult it is to adopt changes. Changes can impact project scope, cost, and time, which in turn can lead to major sources of conflict. A change review process is a very good way to consider changes as rationally as possible. Changes should be avoided unless there are compelling reasons.

Project termination may be appropriate under a variety of circumstances. Sometimes the owner may determine that it is better to stop than to continue. This can be due to changes in the market, cost overruns, or depleted resources. When termination before completion occurs, there are a number of things that still need to be done. Final closeout activities need to be accomplished to ensure that the owner receives whatever he or she is entitled to, and the project team gets their appropriate payment.

There is also a need to coordinate with functional managers of the organization to return those individuals assigned to the project on a temporary basis. Other members of the project team may need to be reassigned, possibly to other projects.

Project Evaluation

Project evaluation is concerned with monitoring progress on a project. The ultimate output of project evaluation is the decision to continue with the project, or to quit. There also is a need for after-action reports, providing a means to learn from the experiences of a project.

Formative evaluations refer to those that are used to control the project. Because projects involve so many interrelated activities, and are undertaken with limited resources, there can be a lot of apparent reasons why a particular activity or work package is not going well. Furthermore, it is very easy for management to think there is a problem when there really isn't.

Meetings are very important in project control. Regular meetings in such an environment are well worth the time taken. There is a need within projects to maintain high levels of communication and coordination. Regularity leads to more thorough preparation on the part of participants. Two commonly used types of meetings used to manage projects are to coordinate activities (usually fairly unstructured) and to reach decisions (usually more structured).

After-action evaluations involve first classifying completed projects into categories of success and failure. Management needs to understand why successful projects worked as well as they did. The reason could be especially favorable external conditions, or could also be due to especially effective implementation by the project team. The key to success is to understand what is true for a given project.

It also is important for organizations that are continuously involved in projects of a given type to gather information about time and cost performance for specific work packages. These work packages should be measured in terms that occur across projects, so that the organization obtains knowledge about what doing a particular bit of work takes. This gives the organization a tremendous advantage over time relative to their competitors either who lack their experience, or who fail to keep similar records.

Multiproject Environments

Many organizations have evolved into organizations that manage projects as the focus of their business. This has long been true in the construction industry, where firms develop skill and equipment expertise that can be applied to a type of work, giving them competitive advantage. It has also been true for a long time in the accounting field, where large firms develop a pool of experts in various fields that can be utilized on the problems of many firms. Information system project management has evolved from the accounting field, with many firms offering expertise that is available for hire. This is probably the most common form of outsourcing, applying expertise from consulting firms for specific problems within organizations. The matrix form of organization is especially appropriate in this environment, with pools of experts trained to a high state of development in their specialty, available on call to cope with work as it is acquired.

Both in information systems and in other fields such as construction, the vast majority of projects occur in a multiple project environment. Projects in this environment tend to be smaller than projects found in other environments. The reason for dealing with multiple projects is to share key resources, which would otherwise be underutilized. Critical resources of this type would be the bottlenecks that make sense to use as the top priority in scheduling. The scheduling of projects subject to resource smoothing was discussed in Chapter 7. In addition to the complications involved with scheduling critical resources, there are additional sources of change in multiple project environments. As new projects are obtained, and old projects encounter difficulties, the priority for use of critical resources is liable to change. For instance, a key production crew might have originally been scheduled to work on a project for the first three weeks in March. After one of these weeks work was completed, an emergency requirement might arise where this crew could help. Top management has the decision of disrupting this current project to fix problems on the project with the emergency. It often makes economic sense to have one project suffer for the greater good of the firm overall. Management is responsible to set priorities and determine which projects will receive top priority.

Table 8.2 Project data

Project	Design	Production	Training	Deadline
A	4 weeks (completed)	7 weeks	3 weeks	Week 20
B	3 weeks	5 weeks	1 week	Week 10
C	1 week	4 weeks	1 week	Week 10

To demonstrate the problems involved in multiple project management, assume a consulting firm does work requiring three crews (design crew, production crew, and training crew). To simplify matters, assume the firm does projects involving three activities, performed in sequence. Therefore, for each project, the design crew performs its work, which must be completed before the production crew can start its work, which in turn must be completed before the training crew does its work. Currently the firm has three projects in progress, as shown in Table 8.2.

The current schedule selected by management (showing only 30 weeks) is shown in Figure 8.2.

After the second week, the firm has completed its work as planned, and obtained two new jobs as shown in Table 8.3.

This yields the following updated schedule (Figure 8.3):

	W	e	e	k																										
	1	2	3	4	5	6	7	8	9	10	11	12	13	14	15	16	17	18	19	20	21	22	23	24	25	26	27	28	29	30
Design	C	B	B	B																										
Production	A	C	C	C	C	B	B	B	B	B	A	A	A	A	A	A														
Training					C						B							A	A	A										

Figure 8.2 Initial schedule

Table 8.3 Added projects

Project	Design	Production	Training	Deadline
D	5 weeks	9 weeks	3 weeks	Week 30
E	4 weeks	6 weeks	3 weeks	Week 20

	Week																													
	1	2	3	4	5	6	7	8	9	10	11	12	13	14	15	16	17	18	19	20	21	22	23	24	25	26	27	28	29	30
Design	C	B	B	B	E	E	E	E	D	D	D	D	D																	
Production	A	C	C	C	C	B	B	B	B	B	A	A	A	A	A	A	E	E	E	E	E	E	D	D	D	D	D	D	D	D
Training					C						B						A	A	A				E	E	E					

Figure 8.3 Updated schedule

	Week																													
	1	2	3	4	5	6	7	8	9	10	11	12	13	14	15	16	17	18	19	20	21	22	23	24	25	26	27	28	29	30
Design	C	B	B	B	E	E	E	E	D	D	D	D																		
Production 1	A	C	C	C	C	B	B	B	B	B	A	A	A	A	A	A	D	D	D	D	D	D	D	D	D					
Production 2					t	t	t	E	E	E	E	E	E	E																
Training					C						B						E	E	E	A	A	A					D	D	D	

Figure 8.4 Feasible updated schedule

This plan is infeasible within available resources. Therefore, another production crew, the critical resource, is developed. New people are to be hired and trained, a three-week process (indicated by the letter "t") required before they can begin productive work (Figure 8.4):

In weeks 3 and 4, problems were encountered in the production of project C, which appear to require an additional 3 weeks. This forces rescheduling production for job A. Once training is announced, it can be delayed, but cannot be shifted back, because trainees need to coordinate their schedules. Therefore, training has to be left as scheduled. Rescheduling production for job A to keep it within its schedule shifts production for job E back. Job E is then delayed beyond its deadline. The firm has meanwhile picked up jobs F and G (Table 8.4):

Table 8.4 New jobs in week 3

Project	Design	Production	Training	Deadline
F	2 weeks	5 weeks	2 weeks	Week 30
G	4 weeks	7 weeks	3 weeks	Week 30

	Week																													
	1	2	3	4	5	6	7	8	9	10	11	12	13	14	15	16	17	18	19	20	21	22	23	24	25	26	27	28	29	30
Design	C	B	B	B	E	E	E	E	D	D	D	D	D	D	F	F	G	G	G	G										
Production 1	A	C	C	C	C	C	C	C	B	B	B	B	B	E	E	E	E	E	E	D	D	D	D	D	D	D	D	D		
Production 2						t	t	t	A	A	A	A	A	A		F	F	F	F	F	G	G	G	G	G	G	G			
Training								C						B	A	A	A		E	E	E	F	F					G	G	G

Figure 8.5 Schedule in week 3

The schedule now looks like what is shown in Figure 8.5.

At this stage, it is clear that the firm is losing much of its slack resources. Project D will not be completed on time even if everything goes according to schedule (or earlier). After week 6, two new projects (H and I) have been obtained, but project F has been canceled. Training on project C has been delayed for 2 weeks because of trainee scheduling conflicts (Table 8.5).

The revised schedule is shown in Figure 8.6.

We leave the schedule at this point. Projects D, E, and I clearly have troubles meeting their deadlines. At the added cost of training new crews, some of this could be alleviated, but not necessarily at lowest cost. The point overall is that multiple project environments have high levels of uncertainty, as new jobs are acquired (and possibly canceled) that make optimized and densely packed resource schedules highly unrealistic. Here we only hypothesized minor duration extension, whereas in reality, delays

Table 8.5. Jobs added in week 4

Project	Design	Production	Training	Deadline
H	5 weeks	9 weeks	4 weeks	Week 40
I	3 weeks	6 weeks	2 weeks	Week 30

	Week																													
	1	2	3	4	5	6	7	8	9	10	11	12	13	14	15	16	17	18	19	20	21	22	23	24	25	26	27	28	29	30
Design	C	B	B	B	E	E	E	E	D	D	D	D	G	G	G	G	I	I	I	H	H	H	H	H						
Production 1	A	C	C	C	C	C	C	C	B	B	B	B	B	E	E	E	E	E	E	D	D	D	D	D	D	D	D	D	H	H
Production 2						t	t	t	A	A	A	A	A	A				G	G	G	G	G	G	G	I	I	I	I	I	I
Training								C						B	A	A	A		E	E	E				G	G	G		D	D

Figure 8.6 Schedule in week 4

can occur of much greater consequence. Added complications of redirecting experienced crews to priority projects in the middle of work tasks can create additional chaos. Overall, operation in a multiple project environment is an extremely interesting endeavor.

Summary

Project control is a means to guide project efforts toward achievement of project goals. A primary means of control is to compare actual work with planned accomplishments. This requires accurate data collection and efficient dissemination of project reports.

There are many reasons that projects fail. Consideration of the failures of others is needed to increase the probability of success of a specific project. High levels of uncertainty and change require flexible project management. Experience and preparation help increase the odds of project success.

Project risk management needs to be applied throughout the life cycle of the project. Consideration of risk was important when the project was initially considered for adoption, and was implemented by estimating what could go wrong in developing the project. In the organization stages of the project, there are a number of things project management can do to ensure good people are obtained, that estimates are realistic, that contingency options are available should problems arise, and that project components delivered by those outside the project organization are received in a timely fashion and perform to specifications. During the building of the project, original time and cost budgets need to be compared with actual performance to determine whether problems are arising. It is important not only to understand that problems exist, but to plan for ways of dealing with the problems that are identified.

Project control should clearly identify responsibilities for work packages, and use these work packages as the basis of cost accounting. The authorization process ensures that management retains control over the project. There is a need to constantly update projected performances in order that top management has a complete picture, and is capable of making decisions to continue the project based upon sound, objective information.

Project evaluation provides organizations that deal with a continuous stream of projects the ability to develop a database of knowledge by work package. This gives such an organization a tremendous edge relative to competitors unable to do the same. Furthermore, careful analysis of post-action success or failure enables organizations to better understand their work environment.

The problems of managing multiple projects arise in most large organizations. The biggest difference in one large project versus many smaller projects is that in the large project, the project team is able to focus on attaining one set of objectives. In a multiple project environment, scarce resources need to be shared by many competing projects, and hard decisions have to be made to further overall organizational goals rather than focusing on the goals of specific projects.

Current references with respect to controlling multiple projects are referenced.[1]

Glossary

After-action evaluations: Post-project assessment to add to organizational learning.

Assessment: Monitoring project progress to identify problems.

Authorization: Control technique requiring managerial approval before resources are expended on an activity.

Benchmarking: Test of system with representative workload.

Control: Actions taken to keep project on target.

Corrective action: Managerial actions to redirect project effort.

Earned value concept: Standard accounting technique crediting progress with its budget value.

Formative evaluations: Evaluations of critical project elements.

High change threshold: Policy to limit changes to project scope.

Incremental development: System development by iterative partial development followed by user testing to verify functionality.

Mission analysis: Evaluation of system component contribution with respect to organizational needs and objectives.

Performance standards: Specifications of a successful project (what the resulting system should do to be called a success).

Pre-award audits: Techniques to assure vendor capacity and reputation.

Prototyping: Testing of a system by developing a small-scale model so that it can be evaluated.

Reference checking: Contact existing users to verify adequacy of system performance.

Requirements Scrubbing: Elimination of unnecessary project elements.

Standard time unit: Work measurement technique identifying typical competent effort needed to perform a specific task.

Technical analysis: Test of the ability of the system to function in appropriate environments.

Variance analysis: Accounting cost control focusing on differences between planned and actual performance.

Work packages: Division of project into groups of related activities.

PMBOK Items Relating to Chapter 8:

3.6 Monitoring and Controlling Process Group—those processes required to track, review, and orchestrate the progress and performance of the project, identify any changes required, and initiate corresponding changes.

3.7 Closing Process Group—those processes performed to conclude all activities to formally complete the project.

4.4 Monitor and Control Project Work—the process of tracking, reviewing, and reporting project progress against the performance objectives defined in the project management plan.

4.5 Perform Integrated Change Control—the process of reviewing all change requests, approving changes and managing changes to deliverables, organizational process assets, project documents, and the project management plan, and communicating their disposition.

4.6 Close Project or Phase—the process of finalizing all activities across all of the project management process groups to formally complete the phase or project.

5.6 Control Scope—process of monitoring the status of the project and product scope and managing changes to the scope baseline.

6.7 Control Schedule—process of monitoring the status of project activities to update project progress and manage changes to the schedule baseline to achieve the plan.

7.4 Control Costs—process of monitoring the status of the project to update the project costs and managing changes to the cost baseline.

8.3 Control Quality—process of monitoring and recording results of executing the quality activities to assess performance and recommend necessary changes.

10.3 Control Communications—process of monitoring and controlling communications throughout the entire project life cycle to ensure the information needs of the project stakeholders are met.

11.6 Control Risks—process of implementing risk response plans, tracking identified risks, monitoring residual risks, identifying new risks, and evaluating risk process effectiveness throughout the project.

12.3 Control Procurements—process of managing procurement relationships, monitoring contract performance, and making changes and corrections as appropriate.

12.4 Close Procurements—process of completing each project procurement.

Reference

1 D.M. Dilts and K.R. Pence. 2006. "Impact of Role in the Decision to Fail: An Exploratory Study of Terminated Project," *Journal of Operations Management* 24, no. 4, pp. 378–396; T.R. Browning and A.A. Yassine. 2010. "Resource-Constrained Multi-project Scheduling: Priority Rule Performance Revisited," *International Journal of Production Economics* 126, no. 2, pp. 212–228.

CHAPTER 9

Project Implementation

In this book, we began with a discussion of the risks involved in accomplishing an information systems project. We then discussed what is involved in information systems project development. We now return to an overall perspective of what is involved in final implementation of information systems projects, with the intent of examining things that can be done to improve a project's prospects of success.

Information System Project Success

Not all information systems projects fail. Care to involve users early in the requirements analysis has proven to be very effective in information system projects. Although there was inevitable variance in the computer literacy of users, the comprehensive and carefully planned training program for the implementation of the new corporate-wide information system led to successful adoption of a more efficient and flexible system.

Information System Project Failure

There are many cases of information systems failing, for a variety of reasons. The implementation stage involves putting the system developed by the project into operation, and turning the system over to the user. The major elements of implementation are system installation and conversion, user acceptance testing, and user training. If testing procedures are cut short as a means of recovering lost time, catastrophic failure often results.

Many information systems projects fail to some degree in terms of meeting design specifications or meeting time and cost estimates. Most project problems are not apparent until late in the project.

Technical validity refers to the system accurately doing the job it was designed to do. Organizational validity has to do with people using the system. Systems can be technically valid, but if there are reasons why users will not use them (such as difficulty in using them), the system will have been a waste. Organizational effectiveness refers to how the system contributes to better performance by the organization. Information system elements are meant to lead to better decision making, but the quality of decision making is impossible to measure except in very narrow contexts. Profit is often used as a measure of effectiveness, but rarely is only one factor responsible for changes in profitability. Probably the best measure of information system effectiveness is its use. Those systems that are used probably are successful, but even those may involve problems.

Four major categories of project system failure are:

- Corresponding failure
- Process failure
- Interaction failure
- Expectation failure

Corresponding failure alludes to the failure of the system to meet design objectives. This is a technical failure in that a computer code did not do what it was intended to do.

Process failure is a failure to bring in a project system on time and within budget. The system may technically work, but it is no longer economically justifiable, or at least not within current business plans.

Interaction failure occurs when a system is not used as much as it was planned to be. This can arise when a system is built to technical specifications within budget and on time, but the intended users do not use it. This can be because of some bias on the users' part to continue to operate the old way, or because the planned system design really did not effectively deal with the problem.

Expectation failure occurs when the system does not quite match up with the expectations of project stakeholders. The system may perform technically, and may be on time and within budget, and may be used, but may not do the job as management was led to expect.

Primary Reasons for Information System Project Failure

Surveys of reasons for information system projects failure consistently identify user involvement as the primary reason, followed by lack of top executive support, and lack of clear statement of business objectives. These traditional critical success factors continue to be cited as the most important.

Lack of Client Involvement

Heavy involvement on the part of users is needed for project success for two important reasons. First, systems analysts need user input to accurately identify the business system, and what business problems are. Second, the project will not work if users do not use the computer system. If the users have been involved in identifying computer system problems, and have been consulted about proposed solutions, there is a much greater likelihood that they will accept the project.

Lack of Top Management Support

Projects have a very difficult time succeeding if they are not "fostered" by top management. Project leadership is important too, but favorable views at the top, with control over purse strings, are probably more necessary for projects to succeed.

That is not to say that support within the project team is not important as well. The implementation team needs to develop team building and cooperation to succeed. Successful team characteristics include a clear sense of mission, understanding of interdependencies of system elements, cohesiveness of the system, and shared enthusiasm and trust within the project team. Within project teams, it is necessary to be flexible. It is also necessary to keep everyone informed.

Although there is no one best leadership style, project managers should have the ability to motivate and inspire. This in great part is due to the fact that they have little coercive authority, especially within matrix organizations.

Table 9.1 Comparison Between Project Managers and Champions

Project Manager	Project Champion
Technical understanding	Cheerleader
Leadership and team building	Visionary
Coordination and control	Politician
Obtain and provide support	Risk taker
Administrative	Ambassador

In addition to the project manager, another key role is the project champion. Project champions often have no authority, but are crucial to the success of projects. A comparison between project managers and champions is given in Table 9.1.

Project champions have been found to be crucial at maintaining interest in information systems projects. This can be very positive, but it can also be negative if counterproductive projects are kept alive after their need has passed. This also has occurred when strong project champions have been present.

Lack of Project Definition

A detailed project plan needs to be developed, defining the system, user requirements, and system requirements. Part of this plan is a clear statement of the business objectives of the proposed system.

The system definition should identify the project team, including its leaders. Team members should be drawn from functional areas. Networks of the flow of information should be developed, along with identification of tasks and their relationship. Budgets need to be established and policies need to be stated.

User requirements include performance measures. These measures are needed to determine the acceptability of the final product. For legal reasons, as well as for operational continuity, it is wise to have good documentation. This documentation becomes the ultimate reference for resolving issues that arise during the project.

System requirements are developed from user requirements. System requirements should clearly state the output of the system in technical terms. Typical information system specifications include:

- Compatibility with the larger system
- Module interchangeability with existing modules
- Cost effectiveness measures
- System reliability standards
- Maintainability procedures
- Test standards

These system requirements are the basis for a detailed list of user requirements and system requirements. Users should review this list to check for accuracy, completeness, and fit with the needs of the organization. Focus on system objectives needs to be maintained.

Quality Control in Project Implementation

Implementation planning involves developing plans and gathering resources to install the system and train users. **Quality control** is an important element in implementing the project.

Study of prior projects was found to improve project quality. A great portion of defects found after delivery were due to insufficient testing of many types of system configurations. Placing the need to obtain higher quality over traditional IBM secrecy, wide participation from customers and outside vendors was obtained in the requirements definition, development, and software testing phases. Written code went through three reviews and four tests. CASE and development support tools were used for development activities. User manuals were edited by professionals at independent editorial service companies. User surveys were used to obtain feedback, and telephone calls made to each customer 90 days after installation.

These steps resulted in an error rate below 1 percent of thousand lines of code at delivery, a significant improvement over prior operating systems. There was a decrease of about 50 percent in customer requests for software assistance. Documentation errors were reduced by 50 percent over earlier projects.

One reason that reported losses on information systems projects are so high is that many projects are canceled late in the project life. This is because most problems are not identified until the testing stage of a project,

Table 9.2 Relative Defect Impact

Stage	Relative cost of defect removal
Requirements definition	1
Design stage	3.5
Coding stage	10
Testing stage	50
After delivery	170

after much of the cost of the project has been expended. Boehm[1] provided relative estimates of the cost of defect removal. For large projects, the ratio of removing defects by phase was estimated to be as shown in Table 9.2.

It is obvious that correcting errors at an early stage is far better than later. To identify errors at early stages, early testing is required. High levels of quality in any operation are obtained by quality inputs, careful production, followed by testing in realistic environments, and user feedback.

User Involvement in Project Implementation

The purpose of **user training** is to teach users how to operate, maintain, and service the new system. Training planning includes identifying the materials needed, personnel to train, and teaching techniques. It is best to involve users in this planning. User approval of the training program expedites successful delivery of material. Training should show how the system fits into the organization's overall information system. All of those users affected by the system should be included in the training program, which should address concerns and show users not only how the system works, but how it contributes to the welfare of the organization.

User acceptance testing is usually required before installation. Ideally, the user organization has been involved in testing throughout the development of the project. This can lead to identification of problems early, so that they do not cause as much damage. If the first user sees of the system is the final acceptance test, failure is almost guaranteed.

Actual installation of information systems can be accomplished in a variety of ways. Alternative strategies include parallel installation, pilot operation, and cold turkey approaches. **Parallel installation** involves running the new system in parallel with the old system. This is the most expensive approach, because the resources required to operate both systems are used. However, it is far safer than other approaches. The **pilot operation approach** involves running the new system on a limited basis. This does not expose the system to a full load. Obvious problems can be identified by this pilot approach, but problems due to workload will not be detected. The **cold turkey approach** is to place a great deal of faith in the new project, pull the plug on the old system, and turn on the new system. This approach is not recommended if it can be avoided.

Training

Some of the reasons training in new ERP systems is difficult include user diversity, the complexity of the new system, and the variety of training methods available. By their nature, ERP systems are going to radically change how many people do their jobs. The theory of ERP is to integrate computer support to all aspects of the business, naturally leading to user diversity. These people are also busy, especially in coping with the requirements of the new system. Training users in new ERP systems can be extremely expensive, often over 10 percent of total ERP system cost.

These points are also of importance to more conventional information systems projects. Although they do not have the pervasive impact of ERP projects, conventional information systems can change how people do their work as well. None of us appreciate having complex new systems thrown at us, without guidance as to how to use them, and understanding what is supposed to get better because we use them.

Experience has demonstrated to companies the importance of training. The most traditional means of training is documentation, usually in large tomes that are never read. For simple systems, such as web sites, traditional help-desk personnel may provide all of the training support needed. The need for flexibility in timing and place as well as the need for training in specific functions have made it important to have flexible training delivery means. This has led to an entire industry providing software training for ERP. There are many delivery formats available, including:

- Web-based virtual training
- Computer-based training
- Video courses
- Self-study books
- Pop-up help screens

These same training venues can be used to train users in any software type.

Summary

Four levels of project failure were presented. Studies of both information system project failure and success were reviewed, intending to identify the circumstances that led to failure, and using these bad experiences to identify procedures that can reduce the likelihood of failure. Additionally, a number of studies of information systems project failure were reviewed.

The primary causes of information system failure are lack of user involvement, lack of top management support, and lack of clear system objectives. Critical success factors in information system implementation were found to change with project stages, but to primarily involve motivation of the project team as well as the three primary factors of user involvement, top management support, and clear system objectives.

The decision to outsource is an important "make-or-buy" decision in information systems project management. Outsourcing can access more current expertise in the rapidly changing world of information technology. It is also quite often less expensive and may be faster. However, outsourcing should be applied only for those activities that are not key to organizational strategy.

To avoid information system project failure, a number of things are needed. Implementation planning, early system testing, and user training are required. Quality control should provide assurance of meeting project specifications. New system support and education are vital because they encourage the acceptance of new processes and systems. Training users is an important element in project implementation. While successful completion of an information systems project is challenging, the benefits are great.

Recent research in information systems project success and failure are referenced.[2]

Glossary

Cold turkey approach: System implementation by cutting the old system and plugging in the new at one moment.

Corresponding failure: Failure of a system to meet its design objectives.

Expectation failure: Failure of a project to meet its stakeholder's expectations.

Interaction failure: Condition of a system not being used by its intended users.

Parallel installation: Implementation of a system while maintaining the old system until assured that the new system functions appropriately.

Pilot operation approach: Implementation of a system on a small scale prior to cutting the old system.

Process failure: Failure of a project to meet time and budget requirements.

Quality control: Means taken to assure that designed product quality is present.

User training: Training provided to users to demonstrate what the system will do, and how the users can apply the new system.

PMBOK Items Relating to Chapter 9:

2.2.3 Project success should be measured in terms of completing the project within the constraints of scope, time, cost, quality, resources, and risk as approved between the project managers and senior management.

3.5 Executing Process Group—those processes performed to complete the defined in the project management plan to satisfy the project specifications.

4.3 Direct and Manage Project Work—the process of leading and performing the work defined in the project management plan and implementing approved changes to achieve the project's objectives.

References

1   B.W. Boehm. 1981. *Software Engineering Economics* (Englewood Cliffs, NJ: Prentice-Hall).

2   K. Wright and C. Capps. 2011. "A Survey of Information Systems Development Project Performance," *Academy of Information & Management Sciences Journal* 14, no. 1, pp. 87–105; R.C. Mahaney and A.L. Lederer. 2011. "An Agency Theory Explanation of Project Success," *Journal of Computer Information Systems* 51, no. 4, pp. 102–113.

References

Aaltonen, K. 2011. Project stakeholder analysis as an environmental interpretation process. *International Journal of Project Management 29*(2), 165–183.

Batra, D., Xia, W., VanderMeer, D., & Dutta, K. 2010. Balancing agile and structured development approaches to successfully manage large distributed software projects: A case study from the cruise line industry. *Communications of the Association for Information Systems 27*, 379–394.

Boehm, B.W. 1981. *Software Engineering Economics.* Englewood Cliffs, NJ: Prentice-Hall.

Browning, T.R., & Yassine, A.A. 2010. Resource-constrained multi-project scheduling: Priority rule performance revisited. *International Journal of Production Economics 126*(2), 212–228.

Cha, C.R. 2014. *Selected Defense Programs Need to Implement Key Acquisition Practices.* GAO-14-309 Defense Major Automated Information Systems.

Day, B., & Lutteroth, C. 2011. Climbing the ladder: Capability maturity model integration level 3. *Enterprise Information Systems 5*(1), 125–144.

Dilts, D.M., & Pence, K.R. 2006. Impact of role in the decision to fail: An exploratory study of terminated project. *Journal of Operations Management 24*(4), 378–396.

Ghapanchi, A.H., & Aurum, A. 2012. The impact of project capabilities on project performance: Case of open source software projects. *International Journal of Project Management 30*(4), 407–417.

Ghapanchi, A.H., Tavana, M., Khakbaz, M.H., & Low, G. 2012. A methodology for selecting portfolios of projects with interactions and under uncertainty. *International Journal of Project Management 30*(7), 791–803.

Jetu, F.T., & Riedl, R. 2012. Determinants of information systems and information technology project team success: A literature review and a conceptual model. *Communications of the Association for Information Systems 30*, 455–482.

Mahaney, R.C., & Lederer, A.L. 2011. An agency theory explanation of project success. *Journal of Computer Information Systems 51*(4), 102–113.

Nunes, N., Constantine, L., & Kazman, R. 2011. iUCP: Estimating interactive-software project size with enhanced use-case points. *IEEE Software 28*(4), 64–73.

Olson, D.L. 2004. *Introduction to Information Systems Project Management,* 2nd ed. Englewood Cliffs, NJ: McGraw-Hill/Irwin.

Peng, W., & Huang, M. 2014. A critical chain project scheduling method based on a differential evolution algorithm. *International Journal of Production Research 52*(13), 3940–3949.

Project Management Institute 2013. *Guide to the Project Management Body of Knowledge (PMBOK Guide)*, 5th ed. Newtown Square, PA: PMI.

Simon, P. 2010. *Why New Systems Fail: An Insider's Guide to Successful IT Projects.* Independence, KY: Cengage Learning.

Symons, C. 2012. Exploring software project effort versus duration trade-offs. *IEEE Software 29*(4), 67–74.

Winch, G.M. 2014. Three domains of project organizing. *International Journal of Project Management 32*(5), 721–731.

Wright, K., & Capps, C. 2011. A survey of information systems development project performance. *Academy of Information & Management Sciences Journal 14*(1), 87–105.

Index

OTHER TITLES IN THE PORTFOLIO AND PROJECT MANAGEMENT COLLECTION

Timothy Kloppenborg, Editor

- *Strategic Leadership of Portfolio and Project Management* by Timothy J. Kloppenborg
- *Project Strategy and Strategic Portfolio Management: A Primer* by William H.A. Johnson and Diane Parente
- *The Power of Design-Build: A Guide to Effective Design-Build Project Delivery Using the SAFEDB-Methodology* by Sherif Hashem

Business Expert Press has over 30 collection in business subjects such as finance, marketing strategy, sustainability, public relations, economics, accounting, corporate communications, and many others. For more information about all our collections, please visit www. businessexpertpress.com/collections.

Announcing the Business Expert Press Digital Library

Concise e-books business students need for classroom and research

This book can also be purchased in an e-book collection by your library as

- a one-time purchase,
- that is owned forever,
- allows for simultaneous readers,
- has no restrictions on printing, and
- can be downloaded as PDFs from within the library community.

Our digital library collections are a great solution to beat the rising cost of textbooks. e-books can be loaded into their course management systems or onto student's e-book readers. The **Business Expert Press** digital libraries are very affordable, with no obligation to buy in future years. For more information, please visit **www.businessexpertpress.com/librarians**. To set up a trial in the United States, please contact **Adam Chesler** at adam.chesler@businessexpertpress.com. For all other regions, contact **Nicole Lee** at nicole.lee@igroupnet.com.

CPSIA information can be obtained
at www.ICGtesting.com
Printed in the USA
LVOW03s0318020917
547271LV00005B/25/P